Intellectual Property Overview and Strategies for Entrepreneurs

A SILICON VALLEY PERSPECTIVE

CECILY ANNE O'REGAN, JD, LLM
PATRICK T. O'REGAN JR., JD, MBA, LLM

DEDICATION

For our parents – it all starts with them.
For all the entrepreneurs and students we've worked with over the years who
helped us hone our craft of teaching and counseling. You all made this book
possible.

A portion of the proceeds of the book will support projects of
Rotary International and our Rotary Club,
the Palo Alto University Rotary Club.

Rotary International is the largest service organization in the world with over
1.2 million members in over 32,000 clubs in 200 countries. Rotary brings
together neighbors, community leaders and global citizens for common good.
Rotary is most known for its efforts to bring about worldwide polio eradication.
However, Rotarians are active in their community and internationally on
diverse projects. Most projects fit within one of Rotary's six areas of focus:
promoting peace, preventing disease, providing access to clean water and
sanitation, enhancing maternal and child health, improving basic education and
literacy, and helping communities develop.

ISBN: 1540527093
ISBN-13: 978-1540527097

TABLE OF CONTENTS

PRAISE FOR IP OVERVIEW AND STRATEGIES

The single most underappreciated and least understood strategic responsibilities of a startup is IP Protection. Cecily and Patrick O'Regan have clearly and concisely delivered descriptions, strategies and checklists that are a must for the serious entrepreneur. By thoroughly incorporating the knowledge presented, founders, management and investors can maximize the value of their ventures.
>   David Epstein, MSEE, MBA, Investor, Coach, and Strategic Advisor for early stage companies with Epstein Advisors, Adjunct Faculty of Entrepreneurial Management at the University of San Francisco

An easy and actionable read of how to protect the intellectual property of a young startup. Cecily and Patrick over the years have dedicated themselves helping entrepreneurs from all world regions. Their book is a manifesto and a practical guide of your next IP protection steps.
>   Carlos S. Baradello, PhD, Managing Partner, Sausalito Ventures, General Partner, Alaya Capital Partners, Professor of Global Innovation & Entrepreneurship, HULT International Business School

Intellectual Property: Overview and Strategies for Entrepreneurs is very accessible to the lay person and opens the reader's eyes to the critical importance of what they may not know about creating and protecting their own intellectual property, including the need to consider third party IP. This is a great introduction to the terminology and complexities of building a successful IP strategy.
>   Jean L. Batman, Esq., founder of Legal Venture counsel and author of the ABA Best Seller Advising the Small Business: Forms and Advice for the Legal Practitioner.

This book is a great source of information to assist all: from experienced Business Development professionals to start ups in the area of intellectual property strategy. It provides a wealth of information to assist you in this important field. It is obvious that Cecily and Patrick have a deep understanding of the subject matter.
>   Mark J. Stephenson, Chief Product Officer, HydroVirga, Inc.

DISCLAIMER

These materials are intended to provide an overview of intellectual property (IP) and IP related strategies and issues that are often relevant to entrepreneurs and start-up companies. The information provided is not legal advice and is not intended to replace consultation with a qualified IP professional. Bear in mind that the law is constantly changing. The information represents our personal views based on the current state of the law in the US and does not represent the views of any employer or client. Rather the information is intended to help entrepreneurs and start-up companies be more knowledgeable about IP rights and associated processes so that they can engage more meaningfully with their qualified IP attorneys and patent agents. Qualified attorneys and patent agents should always be consulted for specific recommendations relevant to the actual facts encountered by an enterprise in their jurisdiction.

ACRONYMS

AEA	Atomic Energy Act
AIA	Leahy-Smith American Invents Act signed into law September 16, 2011
EPO	European Patent Office
IDA	International Development Act
IP	Intellectual Property
IPR	Intellectual Property Rights
IPRP	International Preliminary Report on Patentability
PCT	Patent Cooperation Treaty
PPH	Patent Prosecution Highway
TVA	Tennessee Valley Authority
US	United States
USD	U.S. Dollar
USPTO	United States Patent and Trademark Office
UTM	Utility Model Patent
WIPO	World Intellectual Property Office

CHAPTER 1: INTRODUCTION

Why an Intellectual Property Strategy is Important

IP is an important component of developing a sustainable competitive advantage and can be a key driver of valuation for technology companies. Thus, focused and cost-effective development of an IP portfolio should be considered early on and at regular intervals for most companies regardless of technology. As a general rule, it is always better to make a business decision whether to pursue IP protection, after considering the cost vs. the benefit to the business, over having the decision made for the enterprise due to action or inaction for failing to consider the IP question.

An important benefit of a strong and well-reasoned IP strategy is that it provides an opportunity to exclude others in the commercial marketplace from exploiting the IP and often provides a competitive business advantage. For small to medium sized companies, this strategic business advantage often becomes a key component to investment or acquisition as well as valuation. Moreover, it is a prudent business practice to assess whether

> *Consider the IP question early in the process to avoid IP rights being destroyed by disclosure.*

technology under development is free from the intellectual property rights (IPR) of others.

1

If an enterprise fails to identify and adequately protect commercially useful IPR, the ability to gain a competitive business advantage may be diminished or, in a worst-case scenario, lost. For example, in the situation where a product is manufactured and sold without considering whether IPR are warranted for various product features, the ability to obtain any level of exclusivity with respect to those product features may be lost upon commercialization.

Additionally, it should be noted that with respect to patents most countries in the world operate on an "absolute novelty" basis. In most instances, "absolute novelty" is destroyed upon commercialization of a product or service, publication, or public presentations if a patent application has not been filed before the disclosure. There are some exceptions to this "absolute novelty" rule, which can be evaluated on a country-by-country basis. However, entrepreneurs should operate on the assumption that novelty will be lost when there is public disclosure. Once novelty is lost, the end result could be that the patentable subject matter is placed into the public domain and available to competitors to incorporate into their own products and services with impunity.[1] This ability to incorporate the unpatented

---

[1] Notably the United States has a one year grace period to file a patent application after public disclosure or offer for sale. However, under the first-to-file rules, an earlier filed application could still negatively impact the ability to secure a patent for the disclosed invention. Other countries may provide some limited grace period depending on the circumstances around the disclosure.

technology can also make any regulatory processes easier for a competitor than it otherwise might have been.

Moreover, if an enterprise fails to understand the IPR landscape before making or selling a product or offering a service, it also increases the likelihood that it will be subject to an infringement lawsuit. In contrast, thoughtful consideration of existing IPR and the IPR of other entities enables design parameters or processes to be adjusted during the development phase thereby reducing the likelihood of litigation.

Understanding the IPR landscape can also allow an enterprise to identify potential gaps in the competitor's IP portfolio. With such an understanding, the enterprise can pursue IP rights directed to those gaps and potentially force the competitor into a cross-licensing scenario or obtain more favorable licensing terms, should licensing become necessary. **Appendix A** is an IP strategy checklist which lists some of the issues that should be considered at various points during the development of the product and launching the company.

CHAPTER 2: INTELLECTUAL PROPERTY OVERVIEW

More than Just Patents

IPR are a system of rights designed to provide an incentive for technology development which in turn leads to innovation and technology diffusion. IPR are jurisdictional in nature and serve to protect rights within the jurisdiction in which the rights are protected. It is important to remember that IPR cover a wide variety of IP and are not limited to high technology companies. IPR categories include:

- Patents: utility patents, utility model patents, plant patents, design patents
- Trademarks: trademarks, service marks, trade dress
- Copyright
- Trade Secret
- Sui Generis Rights: database protection; plant variety protection; mask works; traditional knowledge

Each of the potential IPR available to an enterprise based on their business strategy and commercialization efforts, both domestically and internationally, should be considered to ensure the enterprise is fully benefiting from available IPR or knowingly placing IPR into the public domain.

The different types of IPR can be thought of as puzzle pieces which are selected to provide the broadest coverage. Review of IPR strategy can be performed by founders in an early stage

4

enterprise or more formally during an IP committee review for larger enterprises.

One question that arises frequently from students and new entrepreneurs is: *I heard that I can get a 'poor man's patent' or a 'poor man's copyright' by mailing myself a copy of a write-up of the invention.* The origins of this idea may stem from the fact that the United States was, until March 16, 2013, a first-to-invent country and if an inventor had evidence of prior inventorship that inventor would be granted any patent that issued over the inventor that developed the idea later in time. Evidence would need to be sufficient to be scrutinized by a trier of fact and difficult to falsify. One can only surmise that this concept morphed in popular culture into the notion that an inventor or author could have a poor man's patent or poor man's copyright by mailing themselves a copy of the material to be protected. Presumably the post mark is evidence of the date that the invention or authored material was in

> *How about the Poor Man's Patent/ Copyright, you ask? There is no such thing!*

possession of the person. It would be a waste of space to go into the many reasons why this is not the case. Suffice it to say -
THERE IS NO POOR MAN'S PATENT AND THERE IS NO POOR MAN'S COPYRIGHT. [2]

---

[2] *See*, http://www.copyright.gov/help/faq/ *"I've heard about a 'poor man's copyright.' What is it?"*

CHAPTER 3 IP TYPES, ADVANTAGES AND COVERAGE

Utility Patents

Utility Patent
> Protects: New, useful, and nonobvious advances in technology
> Term: 20 years of protection (with possible limited extensions)
> Formalities: Requires a written application in each country
> Also: Some countries provide for *utility model protection* as well which has less stringent review and a shorter term (in the range of 10 years)
> But: Many countries require absolute novelty (i.e., patent application on file before disclosure, use or sale); extent of available coverage may vary from country-to-country (e.g., stem cells, software, methods, traditional or indigenous knowledge, etc.)

The first piece of the IP puzzle to consider is the utility patent. A utility patent application contains several sections designed to place the public on notice of the new and novel features of an invention. Once issued, a patent confers the right to exclude others from making, using and selling a product or service covered by the claims of the issued patent in that jurisdiction. Importantly, a patent does not include the affirmative right to make, use or sell as there might be dominant patent rights in existence or regulatory restrictions (as is the case for medical devices and pharmaceuticals which require separate governmental approval).

In the United States, any "new and useful process, machine, manufacture, or composition of matter, or any new and useful improvement thereof" can be patented.[3] The United States

---

[3] 35 U.S.C. 101.

Supreme Court famously stated *"anything under the sun that is made by man"* is patentable which has led to an expansive view of what constitutes patentable subject matter.[4] Foreign entrepreneurs and enterprises should be particularly mindful that patent coverage excluded in their home country might be obtainable in other countries, such as the United States, and should develop their IP portfolio strategy with that in mind. Conversely, United States entrepreneurs need to be mindful that not all types of coverage available in the United States are available internationally.

Generally, the utility patent application includes a background discussion, a short description of figures (if any are provided), a detailed description of the invention (including a detailed description of all figures provided), a set of claims that define the "metes and bounds" of the invention, an abstract, and all figures necessary to understand the invention.[5] Much like a street address defines where someone lives or works, the claims of a patent define the invention that is covered by the disclosure and thus owned by the inventor or the enterprise. Strategically, the claims should be written as broadly as possible without a complete overlap of the disclosure of other patents or references. It should be noted that the more detail provided in a patent claim, the easier the patent claim is for a competitor to design around. So, while

---

[4] *Diamond v. Chakrabarty*, 447 U.S. 303 (1980), which recognized that genetically modified organisms could be patented in the United States.
[5] *See, e.g.,* 35. U.S.C. § 112, and 37 C.F.R. § 1.71.

7

extensive detail and alternatives are provided in the specification, the claims themselves should be kept as short as possible.

The background section often provides a logical place to describe the current state of the art and any shortcomings, and, for medical device patents, relevant anatomy, disease state and current procedures or treatment modalities. In general, in the United States it is typically recommended that a detailed discussion of prior patents and publications which attempts to characterize the disclosure of the references not be provided. In contrast, other jurisdictions will expect a brief summary of the references and how they are different from the disclosure.

As a general rule, the detailed description of the patent application should disclose currently contemplated commercial embodiments along with any alternate embodiments or design changes that might be implemented by a potential competitor in an effort to "design around" the disclosure while still achieving the same, or a substantially similar, result. This broad disclosure will provide the most flexibility when

> *To maximize value, the Patent should describe your invention along with potential design arounds and consider potential future markets.*

prosecuting the patent application before the U.S. Patent and Trademark Office ("USPTO"). There is no requirement that the disclosed subject matter have been built prior to filing. Dimension ranges can also be helpful in some situations and should probably be included as a general rule. Additionally, drawings should be provided for each view (top, bottom, side, perspective, cross-sections, expanded, etc.) of the device (or devices), as well as the device as finally constructed. Flow charts illustrating method steps should also be provided. For medical device disclosures, it is also prudent to provide figures that illustrate the device in context of the anatomy. Orientation of the device and description of the anatomical axes and planes can also be quite useful. Care should be taken to ensure that correct reference is made to the relevant planes and operation within a range of planes or about various axes.

In the United States, an applicant has been required to disclose the best way ("best mode") of making or using the invention that is known to the inventor(s) at the time of filing the patent application in order to avoid having the patent invalidated.[6] Under the Leahy-Smith American Invents Act (AIA), signed into law on September 16, 2011,[7] that requirement was eliminated for purposes of litigation. However, the Examiner can still issue a rejection of the patent application during the prosecution process on the basis that the best mode was not disclosed or adequate information was not provided to allow others to understand how to use the invention.

---

[6] *See*, 35 U.S.C. § 112.
[7] 125 Stat. 284 *through* 125 Stat. 341.

Utility patent applications have several advantages. A broadly written utility patent application can be crafted so that the claims cover a product currently contemplated by an enterprise, future products, as well as products that might be designed in an effort to develop a competing product. The potential for damage awards during litigation against an infringer is also typically higher with utility patents, although the cost of litigation can also be quite high - particularly in the United States.

> *Lab Notebooks can help establish prior invention when someone has stolen the idea.*

As noted above, the United States is no longer a first-to-invent country. Under the old law, an inventor who could establish an earlier date of developing the idea (conception), with diligent activity towards reducing the idea to practice, could obtain a patent over another inventor who came up with the idea later but filed first. The process of establishing the first-to-invent was determined in an interference proceeding at the USPTO. As of March 16, 2013, the United States now operates on a first-to-file basis.

Establishing the earlier date of the invention was usually achieved by presenting lab notebooks which were maintained, day-to-day by the inventor, signed by the inventor <u>and</u> countersigned by someone who is not the inventor but understood what had been written in the lab notebook. Although the United States is now a first-to-file country, it is still important to keep and maintain lab notebooks. Lab notebooks can be used to establish invention or to prove that derivation of the invention occurred. **Appendix B** provides an overview of good lab notebook keeping procedures. Lab notebooks can also provide useful evidence in the event that an idea was misappropriated.

A utility patent application can also provide the longest term (i.e., duration) for enforcement once a patent has issued. The basic term for a utility patent is 20 years from the earliest effective filing date - typically the date the first utility patent application in a patent family was filed in the United States or the date upon which a Patent Cooperation Treaty ("PCT") application was filed. Additional patent term may be available for Patent Office delay in the United States or for delay in processing the patent as a result of the regulatory review process for the relevant medical device and pharmaceutical products in the United States (and some foreign countries).

When describing medical device inventions, for example, consideration should also be given to: (1) the system and device itself; (2) methods of using the device or surgical methods associated with the device; (3) kits for commercially selling the device; (4) methods of manufacturing; and (5) use the device in a communication network and/or software controlling the operation of the device. Claim sets should be prepared for each applicable commercial scenario and any other commercial scenarios contemplated. For inventions related to pharmaceutical products, similar types of claim strategies should be employed. Bear in mind, however, that most foreign countries, as a matter of public policy, do not allow claims directed to methods for treating a human or animal body by surgery or therapy and diagnostic methods practiced on the human or animal body. [*See*, **TABLE 1.**] Thus, for example, if the lead strategy for IP is based on a surgical method careful consideration of whether meaningful protection is available in a particular jurisdiction should be kept in mind before filing internationally in order to maximize the cost-benefit of the IP portfolio.

Additionally, many countries do not allow software patents without some illustration of a technical effect achieved by use of a machine (a requirement in Europe, for example). Availability of patent coverage for software in a particular country should be considered before filing. The United States still allows software patents for computer programs, but the software needs to do more than operate on a generic computer and the claims need to define more than an abstract idea. [8] For software patents, it is important to provide detail about the technical improvements the software achieves.[9] Abstract ideas can include: fundamental economic practices, methods of organizing human activities, mathematical

---

[8] In *Alice Corp. v. CLS Bank*, 134 S. Ct. 2347 (2014), the U.S. Supreme Court set forth a two-part test to determine patent eligibility. The first part of the test looks at whether the claims are directed to an abstract idea; the second part of the test looks at whether the claims define "significantly more" than an abstract idea.

[9] In *Clarilogic, Inc. v. Formfree Holdings Corp.*, CAFC 2016-1781 (March 15, 2017), the court held that "absent any limitation to how the data are changed, there is little, if any, transformative effect. Data are still data."

relationships, collecting and analyzing data (without more), and
business methods .

TABLE 1

Overview of Claim Availability in Selected Countries†

Country	Surgical Method/Treatment of the Human Body Claims?	Computer Programs?*
UNITED STATES	YES	YES
AUSTRALIA	YES	YES
AUSTRIA	NO	NO
BELGIUM	NO	NO
BRAZIL	NO	NO
CANADA	NO	NO
CHINA	NO	NO
COLOMBIA	NO	NO
CZECH REPUBLIC	NO	NO
DENMARK	NO	NO
EURASIAN PATENT††	YES	NO
EUROPEAN PATENT†††	NO	NO
FINLAND	NO	NO
FRANCE	NO	NO
GERMANY	NO	NO
GREECE	NO	NO
HUNGARY	NO	NO
ICELAND	NO	YES
INDIA	NO	NO
IRELAND	NO	NO
ITALY	NO	NO
JAPAN	NO	YES
NORWAY	NO	YES
POLAND	NO	NO
RUSSIAN FEDERATION	YES	NO
SOUTH KOREA	NO	NO
SPAIN	NO	NO
SWEDEN	NO	NO

TABLE 1

Overview of Claim Availability in Selected Countries†

Country	Surgical Method/Treatment of the Human Body Claims?	Computer Programs?*
SWITZERLAND	NO	NO
TAIWAN	NO	NO
UNITED KINGDOM	NO	NO

†This chart provides general guidance only as to the claim types available in select countries generally of interest to start-up companies. For current coverage, applicants should confer with patent counsel.

* **NOTE**: while computer programs may not be patentable *per se*, computer implemented inventions providing a technical contribution may be patentable or computer implemented inventions that lead to a technical effect may be patentable in some jurisdictions notwithstanding a "NO" indication in this table. Don't forget to consider whether design patent coverage should be pursued for the interface.

††Countries covered by the Eurasian Patent currently include: Turkmenistan, Republic of Belarus, Republic of Tajikistan, Russian Federation, Republic of Kazakhstan, Republic of Azerbaijan, Kyrgyz Republic, Republic of Moldovo, Republic of Armenia. Current country coverage is available at: http://www.eapo.org/en/

†††Countries covered by the European Patent currently include: Albania, Austria, Belgium, Bulgaria, Switzerland, Cyprus, Czech Republic, Germany, Denmark, Estonia, Spain, Finland, France, United Kingdom, Greece, Croatia, Hungary, Ireland, Iceland, Italy, Liechtenstein, Lithuania, Luxembourg, Latvia, Monaco, Macedonia, Malta, Netherlands, Norway, Poland, Portugal, Romania, Serbia, Sweden, Slovenia, Slovakia, San Marino, Turkey. Current country coverage is available at: http://www.epo.org/index.html

Design Patents

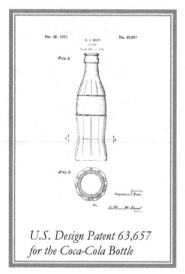

Design patent applications can be an important component to an overall IP strategy for an enterprise and typically may be pursued in addition to the utility patent. Design patents protect the ornamental, as opposed to useful, features of an article of manufacture.[10] An article of manufacture can include a software application interface. The coverage afforded in a design patent is limited to what is shown in the illustrations accompanying the design application and the term is substantially shorter than a utility patent.

U.S. Design Patent 63,657 for the Coca-Cola Bottle

There are several advantages to securing design protection in conjunction with utility protection, particularly in the United States. The test for whether a competitive product infringes a design patent in the United States is an "ordinary observer" test,

---

[10] *See,* 35 U.S.C. § 171.

where the ordinary observer has familiarity with the prior
references. The ordinary observer test requires that the accused
infringing product be compared to the illustrations in the design
patent.[11] While damages typically are much lower than those
available for infringement of a utility patent, design patents provide
a lower cost mechanism for enforcement. Moreover, in the event
of a cross-license of a utility patent, the design patents need not be
included in the license and could ensure that even where a
competitor could practice under the claims of a utility patent, the
competitor could not make a product that looked similar without
running afoul of the rights covered by the design patent.

---

[11] *See, Egyptian Goddess, Inc. v. Swisa Inc.,* 498 F.3d 1354 (Fed. Cir.
2008).

Utility Model Patents (UTM)

Utility Model
➢ Protection functional aspects – a hybrid
  of utility and design coverage
➢ Term: varies by jurisdiction. Ranges
  from 5 years to 15 years
➢ Formalities: requires filing a written
  application in each jurisdiction
➢ BUT not available in all jurisdictions

The Utility Model Patent (also referred to as a "short term" or "petty" patent in some jurisdictions), is not available in the United States, but can provide key benefits to an overall international IP strategy. The utility model protects functional aspects of the invention and provides a right to prevent others from commercially using the protected invention. It should be noted that for the utility model patent application the claim, or claims, are much more limited than a utility patent but more extensive than a design patent. Utility model patent applications typically are not examined, and the term of the patents are often very short (between 5-15 years, depending on jurisdiction). In some jurisdictions, if the claim coverage of the utility model is found to overlap the claim coverage of the utility patent application, an applicant may not be able to secure concurrent rights.

A key advantage of a utility model patent is that it is less expensive to obtain. So, for example, where an enterprise has a limited budget, filing a utility model patent application enables an enterprise to hedge its bets in an emerging market while keeping costs down. [*See,* **TABLE 2**]

17

In an example from China, Chint Group had acquired a
utility model patent for a miniature circuit breaker. Chint then sued
Schneider for infringing its utility model patent. The court ordered
Schneider to pay compensation to Chint group based on the
amount of profits it had earned as a result of the infringement.
Ultimately, Chint was able to secure a global blanket settlement.

TABLE 2
Overview of Utility Model Patent
Protection in Selected Countries†

Country	
UNITED STATES	NOT AVAILABLE
AUSTRALIA	**AVAILABLE**
AUSTRIA	**AVAILABLE**
BELGIUM	NOT AVAILABLE
BRAZIL	**AVAILABLE**
CANADA	NOT AVAILABLE
CHINA	**AVAILABLE**
COLOMBIA	**AVAILABLE**
CZECH REPUBLIC	**AVAILABLE**
DENMARK	**AVAILABLE**
EURASIAN PATENT	NOT AVAILABLE
EUROPEAN PATENT	NOT AVAILABLE
FINLAND	**AVAILABLE**
FRANCE	**AVAILABLE**
GERMANY	**AVAILABLE**
GREECE	**AVAILABLE**
HUNGARY	**AVAILABLE**
ICELAND	NOT AVAILABLE
INDIA	NOT AVAILABLE
IRELAND	**AVAILABLE**
ITALY	**AVAILABLE**
JAPAN	**AVAILABLE**
NORWAY	NOT AVAILABLE
POLAND	**AVAILABLE**
RUSSIAN FEDERATION	**AVAILABLE**
SOUTH KOREA	NOT AVAILABLE
SPAIN	**AVAILABLE**
SWEDEN	NOT AVAILABLE
SWITZERLAND	NOT AVAILABLE
TAIWAN	**AVAILABLE**

TABLE 2
Overview of Utility Model Patent
Protection in Selected Countries†

Country
UNITED KINGDOM   NOT AVAILABLE

†It would be advisable to alert the patent attorney early in the process if utility model protection is of interest, particularly if it is in conjunction with utility protection, to avoid any regional challenges that might exist. A current list of countries providing utility model protection is available at:

http://www.wipo.int/sme/en/ip_business/utility_models/where.htm

Another advantage is that a utility model patent can, in some jurisdictions, be obtained in parallel with a utility patent application. As the utility model patents are often subject to a less expensive litigation process, the utility model patent can be used to assert a patent infringement claim at a lower cost. In those situations, parallel utility model protection may be worthwhile in jurisdictions where there is significant R&D, manufacturing or sales, or where there are concerns that litigation might eventually occur. In Europe, for example, parallel utility model protection for medical device inventions may be useful in Ireland and Germany because each country has a significant medical device industry. However, not all countries allow for dual coverage (e.g., a utility patent and a utility model patent).

Copyright

In general copyright protects expression - in contrast patents protect new and useful process, machine, manufacture, or composition of matter. Thus, for example, copyrights do not protect the underlying facts (or abstract ideas), but it does provide a right to exclude others from copying the expression of those ideas. As with patents, the right to exclude does not include the right to use (as there might be dominant rights). The rights in copyrighted materials begin to accrue when the expression is fixed in a tangible form of expression. Unlike patents, a request for formal registration is not required for rights to accrue. Marking is not required, but is recommended. Suitable marking includes: © [Year(s)] [Owner Name - individual or company]. Additionally, marking can also include other restrictions, for example: "All rights reserved. Reprinted with permission. Further distribution prohibited."

> *Copyright marking is not required, but is recommended.*

It is important to note that while copyright is generally an economic right in the United States and common law countries, in other countries moral rights may also attach. Additionally, in some instances, an independent right of the author to claim authorship and to control "distortion, mutilation or other modification of ... [the] work"[12] also exists. In some countries, the author may even have the right to reclaim possession of the copyrighted work.

In the United States, copyrightable materials created during the course of employment are generally created as "works for hire" unless there is an express agreement to the contrary.[13] This enables the enterprise to be the "author" of the copyrighted materials.[14] Although, there is a general rule, the actual facts in a given scenario may enable a different result and counsel should be consulted to assess whether a work actually qualities as a work made for hire. Clear agreements, whether employment or consulting, establishing the ownership intention is highly recommended.

Copyright infringement occurs when the copyrighted material is copied. In the United States there is a "fair use" exception.[15] Fair use typically falls into two categories: commentary and criticism, or parody. An educational purpose alone does not

---

[12] Berne Convention, Article 6.
[13] 17 U.S.C. 101 provides a definition for what is considered a "work made for hire;"
[14] 17 U.S.C. 201(b).
[15] https://www.copyright.gov/fair-use/more-info.html

necessarily fall within a fair use exception. The fair use exception has limited applicability in the business setting and guidance should be obtained if there is any doubt.

Trade Secret

Trade Secret
- Protects: Information, not generally known, that has independent economic value
- Term: Potentially indefinite protection
- Formalities: No formal registration required in U.S.
- *But*: Requires secrecy and an effort to maintain the information in confidence (e.g. use of Confidentiality Agreements)

Trade secret protects information that can be described with particularity and is separate from matters of general knowledge in the trade. Trade secret also derives an independent economic value from not being generally known. This information could include anything from customer lists to formulas to manufacturing processes to business strategies. The formula for the Coca-Cola® beverage is a quintessential example of a trade secret and illustrates how valuable a trade secret can be to an enterprise. Trade secrets can potentially be protected indefinitely.

Information can provide a competitive advantage when it is kept secret.

A trade secret generally has three components: (1) information; (2) reasonable measures have been taken by the enterprise to protect the information; and (3) information derives independent economic value from not being publicly known.[16] Trade secret in the United States has largely been governed by state

---

[16] 18 U.S.C. 1839.

law. However, a federal trade secret law was enacted May 11, 2016.[17]
Enterprises should work with their local IP attorney/agent or
corporate counsel to develop best practices for trade secret
protection for their enterprise in their jurisdiction.

In general, though, enterprises should ensure that
reasonable efforts are undertaken to maintain the secrecy of the
enterprise's information, particularly if it provides a competitive
advantage. As applied to products, trade secrets generally
encompass features that cannot be reverse engineered. As applied
to the business enterprise generally, trade secret encompasses
information that gives the business a competitive advantage which
includes everything from internal processes to customer lists.

Reasonable steps enterprises should consider to protect
trade secrets include, but are not limited to, for example:

- Limit access to trade secret information.
- Obtaining signed confidentiality agreements and non-
  compete agreements with all employees, and people having
  access to trade secrets, requiring them to protect the
  information *indefinitely.*
- Mark hard copies and soft copies of documents as
  confidential.

---

[17] 18 U.S.C. 1836.

- Keeping copies of trade secret material in a secure physical environment (e.g., by use of fences, locked doors, security guards, restricted areas, etc.).

- Use security systems and access restrictions for personnel (e.g., ID badges).

- Use visitor badges, escorts and sign-in procedures for visitors.

- Use notices (e.g., no trespassing signs, restricted area signs, document/binder/container "Confidentiality" labels).

- Use and enforce rules and practices (e.g., materials locked-up when not in use, clear desk practice, distribution on a "need to know" basis, authorized user lists, copy numbers, distribution logs, etc.).

- Maintain computer and network security (e.g., by encrypting data, using passwords, requiring strong passwords, changing passwords periodically, secure transmission/reception, anti-virus/spyware measures, transmission, copying and printing restrictions, etc.).

- *Promptly* investigating suspected misappropriation.

- Communicating expectation of secrecy to employees who have access to trade secrets.

- Educate employees regarding trade secret.

- Limit access to computer databases and document files on the network.

- Maintain revolving password protection on computer systems and require strong passwords that include numbers, letters and other characters.

- Provide CD <u>burners</u> and USB ports *only* for those who require them.
  - o Consider software that tracks documents copied to USB and provides password protection.

- Require employees to use only company-owned computers.

- Maintain printed materials and specimens in central location with access control.

- Use barcodes or RFID technology to track samples and prototypes.

- Maintain a separate, wholly internal computer system, without Internet or other external network access for most sensitive information.

- Understand how tools on smartphones handle data and, if appropriate, restrict use (e.g., some companies restrict the use of Siri to record ideas because of the privacy policy and the way in which the information is handled).

Additionally, maintaining an audited list of trade secrets may be useful particularly for early stage enterprises. For example, one of the schedules that may be requested during a merger or acquisition transaction is likely to be a list of trade secrets. As with patents, the use of well-maintained lab notebooks can be an important factor in establishing development and protection of a trade secret. Bear in mind that if the trade secret is independently developed (i.e., without theft or misappropriation), there is no recourse. Also, once a trade secret becomes known it is no longer a trade secret.

Trademark, Service Mark, and Trade Dress

Trademarks and Service Marks protect the name of the enterprise and the names associated with the products. Coverage can be sought for words, slogans, designs, pictures, sounds, or any other symbol used to identify or distinguish goods or services in commerce.

A trade dress is available in some jurisdiction and can protect, for example, the distinctive non-functional features that distinguish the goods and/or services in commerce, such as the packaging. The typical term is 10 years and registration can be renewed indefinitely. Typically, only trademarks that are actively being used in commerce are maintained.

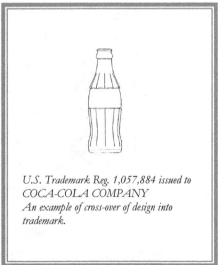

U.S. Trademark Reg. 1,057,884 issued to
COCA-COLA COMPANY
An example of cross-over of design into trademark.

In the United States, both federal and state trademark protection is available. Federal protection can be requested based on actual use of the mark or an intent-to-use the mark. Prior to registration, a statement that the mark is used in interstate commerce (e.g., commerce between states) is provided along with a sample of the mark as used. Interstate commerce in the United States is the date on which the mark was used on goods or services in the sale or transport of goods in between more than one state or US territory, or between the US and another country. For goods, the mark must appear on the goods, the container of the goods, or displays associated with the goods. You may rely on the website where the goods can be purchased via the website.

Once federal registration has been obtained the mark can be used with the encircled R symbol ®. Prior to federal registration, the mark use should be used with ™. As with patents, trademarks are geographic in nature. Therefore, protection in the United States does not extend to protection internationally and separate applications should be filed in those jurisdictions where significant sales are likely to occur. Additionally, it may be appropriate to consider pre-emptive international trademark filings, particularly for emerging markets, to avoid third parties filing for protection and blocking access to the mark in those jurisdictions.

Before launching a company or product, enterprises should have a trademark clearance search performed to ensure that the trademark is available in the jurisdictions of interest.

Translating the mark into various target languages and consideration of the translated meaning is also recommended to ensure that use of the mark in a foreign country does not result in unintended consequences. Marks that are fanciful, such as Xerox® for copiers and Apple® for computers are the strongest marks, while marks that are descriptive are generally not considered trademarkable, e.g., one could not trademark "chair" for a chair or "desk" for a desk. Re-branding a company name and/or its products and services is an expensive endeavor, so clearance and guidance on the name selection is a prudent step and can prove to be cost effective in the long run.

Proper use of the mark is part of protecting the mark as an asset. The trademark identifies the source of goods or services not the actual goods or services themselves. Failure to use the mark properly, or to ensure that others use the mark properly, can result in the mark being declared generic and no longer eligible for trademark protection. For example, when you order a "Coke" at a restaurant you are ordering a carbonated beverage made by the Coca-Cola Company and sold under the registered trademark Coke® and not a Pepsi®. More simply Coke® is a carbonated beverage, a carbonated beverage is not necessarily a Coke®.

Sui Generis IP Rights

Sui Generis IP rights are a legal classification of rights that exist independent of other categories. While countries who are members of the Paris Convention for the Protection of Industrial Property[18] are required to provide a minimum level of patent and trademark rights, and those who are members of the Berne Convention for the Protection of Literary and Artistic Works[19] are required to provide minimum levels of copyright protection, a wide variety of rights (referred to as "sui generis" rights) exist outside these traditional IP areas. Sui generis rights are addressed on a country-by-country basis and are designed to address local needs and concerns, and include, for example, database rights, mask work protection of integrated circuits, plant variety protection and plant breeder rights, supplementary protection certificates (patent term extensions) for patents covering human medicinal products, and traditional or indigenous knowledge.

---

[18] Paris Convention for the Protection of Industrial Property, first signed 1883. Full text available at
http://www.wipo.int/treaties/en/ip/paris/trtdocs_wo020.html ;
countries that are parties to the Paris Convention can be determined by searching WIPO at
http://www.wipo.int/treaties/en/SearchForm.jsp?search_what=C
[19] Berne Convention for the Protection of Literary and Artistic Works, first signed 1886. Full text available at
http://www.wipo.int/treaties/en/ip/berne/trtdocs_wo001.html ;
countries that are parties to the Berne Convention can be determined by searching WIPO at
http://www.wipo.int/treaties/en/SearchForm.jsp?search_what=C

Understanding the Coverage of Available IPR

While there can be some overlap in coverage between different types of IPR, each IPR provides distinct coverage. Moreover, each IPR has its own length, strength and cost. Understanding the various types of IPR available and the costs associated with each type will help an enterprise develop an IPR strategy that provides the best coverage cost effectively. A table of IP protection types is shown in **Appendix E.**

CHAPTER 4: IP STRATEGIES

Focus IP Strategy on Commercially Relevant Features

Product Development and Marketing employees, as well as other functions such as Regulatory Affairs, can often assist an IP Committee understand how a product is being launched, how it is being received by customers (or potential customers), which product features are, or will be, key to achieving a sale over a competitive product, and whether the product is gaining traction in the market. Understanding the commercial information can provide important insight into which technical disclosures should be put through the expensive and time consuming process of filing a utility patent application, and/or maintaining associated trademark registrations. *See,* **Appendix C** which provides a IP Strategy Worksheet and **Appendix D** which is a list of IP related websites of interest to entrepreneurs.

Evaluate Whether to Pursue Trade Secret Protection, Patent Protection or Both

A patent grants the right to exclude others from making, using or selling a product covered under the valid claims of a pending patent for a fixed term as a *quid pro quo* for making the information publicly available. A trade secret, in contrast, is not shared and potentially has an indefinite term. Public policy favors disclosure in a patent over secrecy. However, in some situations, a better business decision might be to pursue trade secret protection as evidenced by the Coca-Cola® recipe example discussed above.

33

Maintaining information as a trade secret, particularly if it is potentially patentable, is a strategy that requires careful consideration by the enterprise and an understanding of the risks and benefits of each type of coverage. In general, if the information cannot be reverse engineered it is a candidate for consideration as a trade secret. However, once the information that was maintained as a trade secret becomes publicly available it loses its status as a trade secret. Moreover, there is a risk that an independent developer could file a patent on the information covered by the trade secret. Also, it should be noted that in some instances, some features can be protected by patent while other features might be maintained as a trade secret.

Preparing a well thought out innovation disclosure submission will assist an IP Review team in determining which type of IP protection makes the most commercial sense. *See,* **Appendix E.**

Defensive and Offensive Patent Filings

Defensive and offensive patent strategies can play a pivotal role in product development. During initial product development, patent strategies are often focused on protecting key market features of the product under development and solutions that might be employed to design around the features. In the United States, even if a patent application issues into a patent, a continuation application, which uses the same specification and figures as the underlying application but presents new claims supported by the original disclosure, can be filed in the United States and several other jurisdictions prior to issuance. The continuation is often used to carve out new and different claims in response to the market activity of competitors. These initial strategies defensively protect the enterprises' right to exclude others from making, using or selling a similar product.

Offensive strategies can be more nuanced and difficult for an enterprise to implement. For example, if an enterprise is attempting to anticipate the direction of a competitor's product development in order to develop blocking IP, chances are that the direction will not be correctly anticipated every time. Additionally, IP can be created to build a link between an enterprise and a potential acquirer or to provide a basis for cross-licensing. These strategies require intimate and ongoing knowledge of the IP of other enterprises and can be particularly important. Having a patent does not shield an enterprise from infringing a competitor's patent, especially if the competitor's patent is broad in scope, but it may provide a cross-licensing opportunity.

Evaluating First Mover Advantage or Defensive Publication over Patents

For some types of development, it may be more cost-effective to forego patent protection in favor of a first mover advantage. This business decision often occurs in the software space where breadth of claims may not be as broad due to the state of the art, where improvements occur at a fast pace, where the

useful life of the technology is short, and where patent coverage
may not be available or is expensive relative to the anticipated
coverage provided.

In some instances, due to cost considerations, an
enterprise may choose to publish an idea rather than pursue patent
protection to ensure that the idea is not patented by another party.
This preemptive publishing enables the information to be used at a
later time, although not exclusively, should strategic plans of the
enterprise changes.

Publication can be achieved in a variety of ways. One
mechanism enterprises can employ is to self-publish (e.g., prepare
white papers that are made available on their website). A drawback
of this type of publication is that it may be difficult to establish an
exact date of publication or to guarantee that the document is
continuously available. Another way to establish a date of
possession of the idea, would be to concurrently prepare a
manuscript and record it electronically with the United States
Copyright Office.

A more reliable way to publish is to publish in a peer-
review journal (which has the downside of putting the actual date
of publication in control of the journal) or use a commercial
disclosure service which charges to publish fully indexed material
submitted.[20]

CHAPTER 5: CONTROLLING THE IP BUDGET[21]

Work with an IP Attorney/ Patent Agent familiar with Your Business Space

IP Attorneys and Patent Agents who focus in your business space will be able to leverage off of their existing knowledge and experience (often making them more efficient and probably less costly regardless of hourly rate) . Moreover, professionals familiar with the business and technical space will have some understanding of the competitive product landscape (making them more creative at claim drafting and better able to identify projects that may not be worth the expense of a patent). Additionally, professionals accustomed to building an IP portfolio with an eye towards investment or acquisition often provide valuable insight into portfolio development from the earliest stages.

While there are benefits to working with an attorney or agent familiar with your technical space, it is not advisable to work with an attorney or agent representing a competitor. The danger of working with an attorney or agent representing a competitor is that confidential information might inadvertently be transferred between companies. Towards that end, it is prudent to provide your attorney or agent with a list of currently known competitors

---

[20] Commercial publication services include, for example, Research Disclosure (www.researchdisclosure.com) and IP.com (www.ip.com).
[21] An excerpt of this section was printed in *"Tips for Getting the Most out of a Bootstrapped IP Budget,"* VentureBeat, October 23, 2009, Cecily Anne O'Regan.

and to update the list periodically. Ideally, the attorney or agent will perform a conflict check for both parties (e.g., competitors) and technology to reduce any risk of information from one client being inadvertently used in another client's patent application.

Focus the patent portfolio on aspects that provide a commercial advantage

Patent applications are not warranted for all inventions. Prepare a matrix of technical improvements against planned commercialization features and types of IP protection available. Rate the importance of the technical improvement to commercialization feature. *See,* **Appendix C**. The patent budget is best spent protecting those technical improvements that provide a competitive commercial advantage over those features that might be a technical improvement but which may not result in additional sales. Additionally, by overlapping IP coverage, costs can be more effectively managed. For example, software can potentially be covered by copyright, patent (some jurisdictions), design patents (for user interface and icons), trade secret (for algorithms), trademark, and database rights (in Europe, to

U.S. Patent 4,022,227 for Method for Concealing Partial Baldness

the extent that the software creates a database of information).

Use Provisional Patent Applications in the United States Wisely and be Mindful of the Potential Pitfalls

Particularly at the earliest stages of an enterprise it makes economic sense to file provisional patent applications in the United States to secure preliminary coverage for inventive concepts. This option may also be available for foreign nationals who are interested in controlling initial filing fees and plan to ultimately pursue their business internationally. *See,* **Table 3** which identifies, for selected countries, whether nationals are permitted to file for patent protection outside their home country as the first filing.

In the United States, filing a provisional patent application first can extend the time and expense for preparing and filing a full utility patent application. Having one or more provisional patent applications on file will also facilitate being able to talk to venture capitalist and angel investors about funding without the risk of running afoul of absolute novelty requirements or disclosure restrictions, especially in connection with international rights. Nonetheless, care should still be taken with respect to disclosure of any information in an unpublished patent application regardless of whether provisional patent applications have been filed. Information concerning early stage filings, in the wrong hands, could provide a basis for another entity to develop an IP strategy around the disclosure which could limit the potential sustainable competitive advantage of the IPR.

Ideally the provisional patent application is prepared as a fully supported application with a complete set of drawings and claims. However, the requirements of a provisional patent application in the United States are much less formal and sometimes it is not feasible to prepare the full utility patent application early. Bear in mind that the provisional patent applications will only provide a basis for support of the claims submitted in the later filed utility patent application if those claims are supported by disclosure in the provisional filing. United States Patent Examiners routinely review the provisional patent application for that purpose and will alter the date that the claims can rely on accordingly. If the claims are not entitled to priority to the earlier provisional patent application, then the Examiner can potentially rely on references dated after the filing date of the provisional application for rejecting the application which could substantially limit the scope of obtainable claims. Additionally, if the provisional patent application does not provide enough disclosure to enable the invention, priority to the earlier provisional patent application will not be granted and intervening references may apply.

Where an enterprise is developing technology across borders (e.g., collaboration on the Internet with inventors located in multiple countries) care should be taken to determine where the IP can be filed. If necessary and available, permission for filing should be obtained in advance of filing. Moreover, a determination that filing a patent application in another jurisdiction (such as the

United States) is not an impermissible export of technology should be made prior to filing.

TABLE 3
Overview of Selected Countries Filing Requirements†

Country	FIRST PATENT APPLICATION MUST BE FILED IN INVENTOR'S HOME COUNTRY? ††
UNITED STATES	YES
AUSTRALIA	NO
AUSTRIA	NO
BELGIUM	NO
BRAZIL	NO
CANADA	NO
CHINA	YES
COLOMBIA	NO
CZECH REPUBLIC	NO
DENMARK	NO
EURASIAN PATENT	NO
EUROPEAN PATENT	NO
FINLAND	NO
FRANCE	YES, for inventions concerning national security
GERMANY	YES, for inventions concerning national security
GREECE	YES, for inventions concerning national security
HUNGARY	NO
ICELAND	NO
INDIA	YES
IRELAND	NO
ITALY	YES
JAPAN	NO
NORWAY	YES, for inventions concerning national security
POLAND	YES
RUSSIAN FEDERATION	YES
SOUTH KOREA	NO
SPAIN	YES

TABLE 3
Overview of Selected Countries Filing Requirements†

Country	FIRST PATENT APPLICATION MUST BE FILED IN INVENTOR'S HOME COUNTRY? ††
SWEDEN	NO
SWITZERLAND	NO
TAIWAN	NO
UNITED KINGDOM	YES, for inventions concerning national security

†Confirmation of the current requirements for filing should be coordinated with counsel in the home country as well as the target country of filing prior to filing.

††Based on residence not citizenship.

International Coverage: Filing Utility Patent Applications under the Patent Cooperation Treaty (PCT) vs. Direct National Filing

Under the Paris Convention, member countries have one year to file their utility patent application in other Paris Convention Countries while claiming the priority date of the earlier filed patent application (the Paris Convention deadline for a design patent application is 6 months). Thus, the later filed patent application can essentially be treated as if it was filed on the first date. Traditionally, this meant that enterprises needed to make the decision about whether to file in Europe or Japan by the 12-month deadline (for utility patent applications). However, since the 1970s Applicants have had the option of delaying that decision by filing a patent application in the World Intellectual Property Office (WIPO) under the PCT. Although a PCT application does not result in an issued patent, filing a PCT application does provide a relatively

low-cost mechanism that enables an enterprise to defer the cost
associated with protecting foreign rights *in most countries* for an
additional 18 months while further information is obtained
concerning the commercial
viability of an invention
internationally.

Patents are geographic in nature. Focus patent filings in countries: (1) with a large market for the product; (2) with significant manufacturing ability; and (3) regional choke points for importing products. Balance this information against ability to enforce patents, once granted.

In developing a
foreign filing strategy,
enterprises should consider
countries with significant
market or manufacturing
ability or potential that may affect the business of the enterprise.
Additionally, the ability to enforce the IP is also an important
consideration.[22] Once those countries are identified, it should be
determined early in the process whether those countries are a
contracting party to the Paris Convention[23] and/or member states
of the PCT.[24] Countries that are not a member of the PCT
includes, for example: Argentina, Taiwan, Saudi Arabia, Kuwait,
Thailand, and Qatar. Additionally, Taiwan is not a member of the
Paris Convention and, unless a country has a bi-lateral agreement
with Taiwan to provide for a 12 month grace period, applications

---

[22] *See*, The Roots of Innovation, prepared by the U.S. Chamber of
Commerce, February 2017 (available at www.uschamber.com)
[23] Paris Convention Member Countries administered by WIPO are listed
at
http://www.wipo.int/treaties/en/ShowResults.jsp?lang=en&treaty_id=2
[24] Member States of the PCT are listed at:
http://www.wipo.int/members/en/

must be filed in Taiwan as soon as possible after filing a first application and before public disclosure.[25]

The PCT process also includes an International Search of available references, publication of the application, an advisory Written Opinion on the patentability of the claims and, if desired, an advisory International Preliminary Report on Patentability (IPRP) which is sent to patent offices of the designated PCT states. The results of the IPRP can be used to further refine claim strategies and/or country selection.

If the PCT application is prepared from a United States provisional patent application, the PCT application must be filed in the Receiving Office for a country where at least one Applicant (usually the company) resides. Thus, if none of the Applicants are located in the United States, for example, a PCT application is not properly filed in the United States Receiving Office of the PCT and will be transferred to the PCT International Bureau.

Prepare Your Own Patent Figures

Several things should be kept in mind when preparing figures for use in patent applications. The cost savings for preparing the figures yourself ranges from $50-$150 per sheet of drawings. However, preparing drawings yourself is not without

---

[25] The United States and Taiwan have a bi-lateral agreement that allows U.S. applications to be filed in Taiwan up to the one year filing anniversary, much like the Paris Convention provision.

risk. While this list is not exhaustive, it covers basic considerations. When preparing drawings keep in mind the following:

1. **Black & White Line Drawings:** Black and white line drawings are the standard. India ink (for hand drawings) or its equivalent are required. *Think "reproducible."*

    a. For drawings prepared with computer programs, such as Visio, a line weight for the device itself should be approximately 5 pt, with weights for lead lines and shading having a weight of no less than 3 pt. The idea is that the lines should be crisp and reproducible during the publication process. *Figures that are difficult to read may result in a new matter rejection during the correction process, thereby potentially causing loss of patent rights.*

    b. Lead lines should have a weight of no less than 3 pt. Arrow head endings are typically used for denoting, for example, a device or an entire section. Lead lines with no arrowhead that touch an element or part are used to identify specific parts of a device.

    c. *No fill or shadowing should be used.* Therefore, traditional CAD models are not appropriate for patent drawings. Removing the fill and adjusting the line weight can make the CAD drawing suitable for a patent filing.

d. As a general rule the drawings should *not include verbiage*; if verbiage is used it should be in 12 point font and should be readable in the same direction as the Figure legend.

e. Part numbers should be at least 12 pt font.

f. The drawings must contain as many views as necessary to show the invention. The views may be plan, elevation, section, and perspective views.

   i. For mechanical items, a perspective view of an entire device is typically shown in one figure.

   ii. Top, bottom, and side views shown in another set of figures.

   iii. Thereafter, as many cross-sections, interior or exploded views as are required to understand the invention are provided.

   iv. Flow charts of methods of use or manufacture may also be provided.

g. Exploded views, with the separated parts embraced by a bracket, to show the relationship or order of assembly of various parts are permissible. When an exploded view is shown in a figure which is on the same sheet as another figure, the exploded view should be placed in brackets.

h. Partial views drawn on separate sheets must always be capable of being linked edge to edge so that no partial view contains parts of another partial view. A smaller scale view should be included showing the whole formed by the partial views and indicating the positions of the parts shown. When a portion of a view is enlarged for magnification purposes, the view and the enlarged view must each be labeled as separate views.

i. Hatching should be used to indicate section portions of an object, and must be made by regularly spaced oblique parallel lines spaced sufficiently apart to enable the lines to be distinguished without difficulty. Hatching may be broken off wherever reference characters are inserted. Hatching must be at a substantial angle to the surrounding axes or principal lines, preferably 45°. A cross-section must be set out and drawn to show all of the materials as they are shown in the view from which the cross-section was taken.

2. **Color Drawings:** When color drawings are required as the only practical way to disclose the subject matter, the color drawings must be of sufficient quality that details are reproducible in black and white in the printed patent. The United States has a mechanism for accepting color figures; foreign jurisdictions may not.

3. **Photographs:** Photographs are not normally permitted, but may be accepted if they are the only practical way to illustrate the claimed invention. The photographs will be printed in grayscale.

4. **Size of Paper:** All drawings must be the same size. A4 (European sized) or Letter Sized (8.5 x 11 inches) can be used. *Drawings submitted in the PCT must be on A4.* So, anything prepared for letter sized paper should be convertible to A4.

5. **Margins:** Each sheet must include a top margin of at least 2.5 cm (1 inch), a left margin of at least 2.5 cm (1 inch), a ride side margin of at least 1.5 cm (5/8 inch), and a bottom margin of at least 1.0 cm (3/8 inch).

6. **Copyright / Mask Works:** A copyright or mask work notice may appear in the drawing, but must be placed within the sight of the drawing immediately below the figure representing the copyright or mask work material and be limited to letters having a print size of 32 cm. to 64 cm. (1/8 to 1/4 inches) high. The content of the notice must be limited to only those elements provided for by law. For example, "©2008 John Smith" (17 U.S.C. 401) and "*M* John Smith" (17 U.S.C. 909) would be properly limited and, under current statutes, legally sufficient notices of copyright and mask work, respectively.

7. **Numbering:** Drawing sheets should be numbered consecutively in the middle of the top of the sheet in the

format "Page#/Total Pages," but not in the margin. The sheet numbering should be clear and larger than the numbers used as reference numbering (e.g., 14 pt or higher).

8. **Figure Numbering**: Figures should be numbered consecutively and be preceded by "Fig." or "Figure" followed by the number. The font should be 14 pt or larger.

Prepare a Realistic Budget

Early stage enterprises are often surprised by the cost of various aspects of obtaining and maintaining IP coverage. Filing a provisional patent application in the United States for a small entity has a fee of $130 for the government filing fee and the cost of the attorney preparing the application - which can vary widely depending on how much time is spent on the provisional, the complexity of the technology, the number of figures, whether or not claims (not required) are prepared and so on. Additionally, an early understanding of the costs associated with the national stage filing should be determined in order to better forecast the budget needs for the enterprise.

A sample budget could be as follows:

	Y1	Y2	Y3	Y4	Y5
Australia			$4,000	$0.00	$0.00
Brazil			$6,000	$800	$800
Canada			$3,500	$1,550	$500
China			$9,000	$0.00	$0.00
Europe			$10,000	$1,100	$1,300
India			$2,300	$600	$0.00
Japan			$12,000	$0.00	$0.00
Korea (South)			$11,000	$0.00	$1,500
PCT		$5,000	$0.00	$0.00	$0.00
Taiwan		$3,000	$0.00	$0.00	$1,500
United States	$5,000	$12,000	$2,000	$0.00	$5,000
TOTAL	$5,000	$20,000	$59,800	$4,050	$10,600

The estimates are based on an application of medium complexity 20 pages in length with five sheets of figures having a single invention disclosed which is filed in the United States as a simple provisional without claims first (Y1), then filed in the United States, Taiwan and PCT as a utility (Y2), with entry into the national stage from the PCT for selected countries (Y3). The foreign estimates include translation costs, filing fees, and estimated foreign associate charges. The estimates for Y4-Y6 take into consideration estimated dates when prosecution of the application would begin in each country, and annual taxes that might be required. As an enterprise files more patent applications and pursues protection internationally, the budget increases accordingly. Additional fees and costs may accrue for other actions, such as change of owner, reporting official communications, and sending reminders concerning outstanding deadlines.

For a spreadsheet of a budget estimator (in USD) that can be manipulated, please contact the authors.

CHAPTER 6 : FAST-TRACK PROSECUTION STRATEGIES

Typically, early stage companies and entrepreneurs prefer to defer patent costs until after funding is secured. However, in some cases having an issued patent in hand quickly can benefit the enterprise. For example, during the process of funding it may be advantageous to have issued patents in hand or where there is an imminent need to enforce the patent. Generally, design patents and utility model patents will issue more quickly than the utility counterparts. Accelerated examination can be requested in the United States based on the following:

- Request that an application be "made special" possible reasons include, for example:
  - Applicant's health
  - Applicant's age
  - Prospective manufacture of a device
  - Actual infringement
- Petition to accelerate can be filed for inventions meeting the following requirements:
  - Invention directed to a *single* invention
  - Submitting a statement that a pre-examination search was performed (listing a detailed field of search)
  - Submitting a copy of each reference that is *most closely* related to the subject matter of the claims along with a

detailed discussion of the references which discusses
how the claims are patentable over the references.

- Patent Prosecution Highway (PPH)
  - Applications filed in the United States from a select
    number of countries within the PPH can also receive
    accelerated examination.[26]
  - Under the PPH, an applicant obtaining allowance of
    claims on file in a PPH country may request that the
    USPTO fast track the examination of corresponding
    claims in the United States. This allows Applicants to
    leverage off of prosecution in another country to
    obtain corresponding patents faster and more
    efficiently.
  - With permission obtained from the USPTO prior to
    filing, a United States Applicant can file in one of the
    PPH jurisdictions as a first country as an option for
    obtaining quicker allowance in the United States
- Request for Track 1 Prioritized Examination[27]
  - Limited to 10,000 applications filed per fiscal year

---

[26] Currently, the USPTO will accelerate applications filed in the United
States claiming priority to applications from Australia, Austria, Canada,
China, Denmark, Estonia, European Patent Office (EPO), Finland,
Germany, Hungary, Iceland, Israel, Japan, Korea, Norway, Nordic (NPI),
Poland, Portugal, Russia, Singapore, Spain, Sweden, and the United
Kingdom. A list of PPH countries is maintained at:
https://www.uspto.gov/patents-getting-started/international-
protection/patent-prosecution-highway-pph-fast-track
[27] See, https://www.uspto.gov/patent/initiatives/usptos-prioritized-
patent-examination-program

- $2,000 fee for small entity
- Limited to 4 independent claims and 30 total claims
- No examination support document required from applicant

Applications which are accorded special status or have been accelerated can potentially result in a patent issuing within twelve (12) months. Overall, though the time for obtaining a patent can run from 3-5 years from earliest filing, depending on technology. *See* **Appendix F** which provides a sample time line and strategies for United States and foreign filing.

CHAPTER 7: IP MONITORING PROGRAMS AND FREEDOM-TO-OPERATE SEARCHES

Timing a Freedom-to-Operate (FTO) Search

It is prudent to perform a preliminary FTO, or a patent landscape review, early in the product development process to identify competitor IP that might be problematic to the design of the product or that has the potential to be problematic (in the case of pending applications). This review can then be used by the R&D team to develop the project without running afoul of the IPR of another entity. As patent documents that are available at any given time were typically filed 18 months earlier, ongoing searching should be encouraged to fill in the gaps for later published applications or issued patents.

Professional searchers (usually former patent examiners) and some foreign Patent Offices offer services that can be used in conjunction with a review by a licensed patent professional in the relevant jurisdiction to identify the most relevant IP for understanding any freedom-to-operate issues. The downside of using such services is that it limits the assurances the attorney reviewing the results can provide as to the thoroughness of the search strategy. However, it can at least provide a cost-effective first step to assessing the IP landscape for a product. Countries that outsource their examiners include: United Kingdom and the Scandinavian countries.[28] Bear in mind that commissioning a

search includes a disclosure of the invention and can be considered
an export of technology if sent outside the United States, which is
not allowed in the United States without a license.

In some cases, it may make sense to monitor the pending
published applications of interest to ensure that future
amendments to the patent applications do not, for example, make
the initially presented patent claim more of a concern.

An updated FTO search and review is generally performed
(leveraging off of earlier searches) at least commensurate with a
freeze in the product design and preparation for manufacture and
then updated again at commercial launch of the product. The
updated searches are geared towards identifying intervening
references that may have become available which should receive
further scrutiny.

Any knowledge of other's IP obligates the enterprise to
submit to the USPTO the information that may be considered to
affect the patentability of the enterprise's pending patent
applications under Rule 56.[29] This process is typically referred to as
an Information Disclosure Statement filing. Failure to cite a known
reference can jeopardize the validity of any patent that issues. The
requirement to cite references can also apply in a foreign countries
as well. For a variety of reasons, it is recommended that an

---

[28] Several foreign patent offices offer search services. This includes, for
example, the Nordic Patent Institute (http://www.npi.int/).
[29] 37 C.F.R. 1.56.

enterprise use outside patent counsel request and process any searches.

Benefits of Monitoring Competitor IP

By monitoring the IP of known competitors, an enterprise can often determine a strategic direction for their product development, albeit with an 18 month lag time from filing to publication, and can form their R&D strategy relative to the competitors earlier in the process. Generally, monitoring of the IP is performed by one of the R&D employees in collaboration with patent counsel.

CHAPTER 8: MINIMIZING LITIGATION RISK

There is no way to completely eliminate the risk of IP related litigation. However, using patent counsel to perform searches in advance and establishing an IP monitoring system will assist in identifying and avoiding problems thereby reducing the risk. Additionally, by knowing about the IPR of others an enterprise can then take reasonable steps to ensure that either products or services offered do not infringe the IPR of others. A formal legal opinion stating that either there is no infringement or the IPR is invalid may also be obtained.

If an enterprise receives a communication advising of the existence of IPR or offering a license to the IPR, *do not ignore it*. Review the communication with your IP counsel to determine the type of response that is appropriate. For small enterprises that are either pre-funded or between funding, the question of whether a communication has been received often arises during due diligence performed by an investor. Having a well-reasoned response and strategy is important and will enhance credibility with a potential investor.

At a minimum, the enterprise will want to carefully consider whether their product/services infringe the IPR. It may make prudent business sense to obtain an opinion from IP counsel outlining why the product/services are not covered by the asserted IPR. Another option may be to have IP counsel evaluate the IPR to determine whether the IPR is even valid. An invalid IPR cannot be successfully asserted.

An additional step may be to write a response to any communication received. In the United States particularly, the benefit of preparing a carefully crafted response is that the response may be used to support an estoppel argument in the event of subsequent litigation. Even if the response comes from the enterprise, it is good business practice to obtain the assistance of IP counsel in preparing the response.

Patent marking can, in the United States provide a mechanism to obtain enhanced damages in the event of patent infringement. However, "false patent marking" has the potential for statutory damages up to $500 per mismarked item.[30] False patent marking can occur by putting an incorrect patent number on the product or by continuing to mark a product with the patent number after the patent expires.

Patent marking activities should be coordinated with IP counsel and good business practices should be developed to reduce the likelihood that a product will be incorrectly marked. In reviewing the patent marking, ensure that at least one patent claim from each issued patent listed on a product (or product label or website) reads on the actual product; use "patent pending" only when a patent application is on file and currently pending; if the

---

[30] 35 U.S.C. § 292.

product changes confirm that new versions of the product continue to be covered by at least one patent claim; note the expiration dates of patents and keep track of the dates with the patent marking information; periodically review and update markings with newly issued patents and remove expired patents; as a general rule review patent marking anytime the product labeling is updated.

Under the AIA patent holders are no longer subject to false marking claims of third parties who have experienced no damages as a result of the false marking. Additionally, the ability to bring false marking cases was made more difficult and the number of lawsuits filed claiming false marking has been substantially reduced. Additionally, patent marking can be performed "virtually" by marking the goods with "Patent" or "Patent Pending" with access to a freely accessible website address.[31]

---

[31] See, for example,
http://www.callawaygolf.com/on/demandware.store/Sites-CG2-Site/en_US/CustomerService-Show?fid=legal&cid=legal-patents

CHAPTER 9: LICENSING

Factors to Consider When Licensing In or Licensing Out

There are several reasons why licensing may become an important part of an overall IP strategy. First, licensing or cross-licensing may unblock interlocking IPR. Licensing can also be used to settle an IP litigation or United States patent inter partes proceeding. From a business perspective, licenses can be used to grow and diversify the business, deal with outside idea submissions and convert dormant IP portfolios into a source of income. Universities and governmental research entities are often an excellent source of foundational IP.

An Assignment transfers all of the rights in the IP, while a license transfers a sub-set of the rights. Licenses can be exclusive or non-exclusive, and can include or restrict the ability to transfer the license. Licenses can be entered into for: patents, trademarks, copyright and/or technology. The rights can be limited by, for example, time, field of use, geography, product, claims (patents), etc. It is important to note that an agreement between parties which is labeled as a license but transfers all the rights to the IP may result in an assignment of the IP.

Generally, the United States Government Does Not Have a License to Infringe

In the United States, governmental entities generally are not supposed to infringe the IPR of others. However, there are situations where the government can infringe. Examples, include, the TVA (Tennessee Valley Authority), the IDA (International Development Act), AEA (Atomic Energy Act), Air Pollution Control, and plant variety protection. All provide for some form of compulsory licensing.

Compulsory Licenses

Some countries provide a mechanism for a compulsory licensing. This is typically required in situations where the patented invention is not being "worked" in the country (e.g., commercially exploited) . Where the potential impact of technology could be important to a country, such as technology relating to climate change in a developing country, special consideration should be given to whether foreign jurisdictions are likely to either require compulsory license for a non-worked invention or require that the patents at issue be placed into a patent pool in order to maximize exploitation within that country as a matter of public policy.[32]

Antitrust Considerations

In the United States Antitrust laws (state and federal) are laws which promote fairness for consumers. [Other countries refer to this as "competition law."] There are two components to antitrust law in the United States. The first is a restriction on forming cartels or engaging in collusive practices that would

---

[32] Compulsory licensing is provided for under the Paris Convention (art. 5) and TRIPs (art. 31).

restrain trade. The second restricts mergers of organizations that would lessen competition.

Agreements between parties can inadvertently trigger antitrust issues if the agreement results in a restraint on trade. Qualified attorneys can help navigate the nuances of legal compliance with these laws.

Business Considerations for the License

When working with counsel to prepare your agreement, the enterprise should be aware of their business objections. A partial list of issues to understand and consider include:

- The role of each party to the agreement
- The business objective to be achieved
- How will the parties combine their expertise
- What kind of agreement is intended: a full transfer (assignment) or a partial transfer (license)
- If a license is contemplated, what kind
  - Exclusive or non-exclusive – i.e., is the person providing the rights able to also contract with other businesses
  - Will there be a royalty – if so, how much and what is the basis
  - What territory will be covered: worldwide, country specific, etc.
- What kind of rights will the licensee have
  - Can the licensee make or sell the licensed item

- o   Can the licensee publicly perform or display
  the licensed item

- o   Can the licensee import or export the licensed
  item

- What kind of restrictions are contemplated
  - o   Is the licensed material for internal use
  - o   Can the licensee sub-licensee or transfer to
    another party
  - o   Can the licensee modify the licensed material
  - o   What is the time period of the license
  - o   Can the licensee combine the licensed
    material with other materials

- Ownership
  - o   Who owns the IP that is subject to the
    agreement
  - o   Who owns any IP that might be developed

- Are there any warranties

- What are the limits to liability

- What are the confidentiality requirements

- Where will any dispute be resolved (i.e., which court)

- Are there minimum damages

- Is any open source software or free software involved

CHAPTER 10: PREPARING FOR IP DUE DILIGENCE RELATED TO A FINANCING EVENT

Some level of due diligence will often be performed on the IPR portfolio in conjunction with a financing event. The level and extensiveness of diligence typically varies depending upon the amount of the financing event and the maturity of the enterprise.

IPR Inventory and Ownership

At a minimum and as a first step, an inventory list of all IPR will typically be requested from the enterprise in conjunction with the financing event. For IPR which has been the subject of a formal application, a list of the applications (which includes the serial number, filing date, title/mark, inventors (for patents)), publication number and date (if available), and registration number/patent number (if available) and date. Additionally, supporting documents such as Filing Receipts and formal Assignments establishing a clear chain of title to the enterprise may also be requested. Having this information and the supporting documents organized and easily

> *Many a founder has been blindsided by an inability to transfer ownership of the IP to the company because a co-founder has left before assigning the IP.*

accessible will reduce the amount of time and money required to comply with the due diligence request. In some cases, a copy of the employment agreement for each key employee or inventor may be required. In the United States, employment agreements are useful for identifying whether an employee has exempted any IP from the obligation to assign IP to the company.

A common mistake that occurs when transferring the IP is to fail to use the legal name of the enterprise as recorded with the governmental agency. For example, a company might refer to itself as "Acme" but the name registered with the Secretary of State is "Acme, Inc." Documents transferring ownership should use the full legal name not the shortened name or trade name.

Patentability and Freedom-to-Operate Review

Additionally, a due diligence request may include a request to review, typically by conference or conference call, any patentability searches, patent landscape reviews, or freedom-to-operate searches. In some cases, counsel for the investor will hire independent counsel to perform supplemental or auxiliary patent searches in conjunction with the financing event.

Claim Scope Review

For patents (issued and pending) investor's counsel may review claims to ensure claim scope broadly covers current product plans with flexibility to encompass future products. Investor's counsel may also perform a review of competitor patents to assess how the enterprise's portfolio compares. This level of review is more often involved when the amount of the investment is over $10M USD.

CHAPTER 11: CONCLUSION

The key to developing an IP strategy is to understand the commercial advantages of your enterprises solution as compared to competitors. From that starting point, enterprises should use more than one type of available of IPR to protect the business objectives. By determining the types of coverage that is available and the aspects of the business that are the most important, a cost-effective IP strategy can be developed.

BIOGRAPHY

Cecily Anne O'Regan is a registered patent attorney with more than twenty years of experience in patent and intellectual property law. Cecily has a B.S. from the University of California, Irvine, a Juris Doctor from the University of San Francisco, School of Law, and an LLM in Innovation, Technology and the Law, awarded with distinction, from the University of Edinburgh (Scotland). Cecily also received a graduate certificate in Biodesign from Stanford University.

Email: coregan@sflaw.com

Cecily's practice focuses on securing worldwide intellectual property protection and related business strategy for emerging technology clients, with particular experience in the medical device and clean technology sectors.

Cecily combines unique legal, academic and business credentials as an entrepreneurial patent professional, with hands-on experience providing strategic, market-focused patent portfolio development and intellectual property advice for clients. She also performs patent due diligence to assess patent portfolios for venture capital investment, mergers and acquisitions, and licensing opportunities.

Cecily is a co-inventor on several patents in the field of medical device technology and software as a service, a frequent business plan competition judge and entrepreneur mentor, and a published author on intellectual property law.

Patrick T. O'Regan Jr. is a licensed US attorney. Patrick has a B.S. from Brown University, a Juris Doctor from Suffolk University, School of Law, an MBA from Trinity College Dublin (Ireland), and an LLM in Innovation, Technology and the Law, from the University of Edinburgh (Scotland).

Email: ptoreganjr@usfca.edu

Patrick is an Adjunct Professor at the University of San Francisco, in the School of Management. Patrick has taught courses in Entrepreneurial Management, Entrepreneurial Finance, and Entrepreneurial Leadership, and a published author on intellectual property law. Patrick also coaches a team of USF MBA students for the Venture Capitalist Investment Competition.

APPENDIX A

IP STRATEGY CHECKLIST

I.   GARAGE STAGE (COMPANY NOT FORMED OR FUNDED)

- ❏ Meet with and select corporate counsel; discuss strategy, cost and timing for formation and associated activities.

- ❏ Identify contributions and expectations of each founder or early participant; work with corporate counsel to prepare written summary of contributions and expectations.

- ❏ Review prior employment agreements of each founder or early participant to ensure that ideas under development for new company would not have a claim of ownership from a prior employer.

- ❏ Perform IP searches to get an understanding of the IP landscape and identify any show stoppers or possible licensing-in opportunities.

- ❏ If applicable, prepare Invention Disclosure forms for patentable ideas related to the enterprise.

- ❏ Meet with and select IP counsel familiar with your business space and working with entrepreneurs to prepare and file patent applications.

- ❏ File patent applications, if possible.

- ❏ Consider other types of IPR that might be available in your home jurisdiction and foreign jurisdictions with a substantial market.

- ❏ Prepare preliminary list of IPR, including trade secret list.

- ❏ Establish trade secret practices.

❑ Obtain signatures on Non-Disclosure Agreements whenever possible and maintain a list of all Non-Disclosure Agreements that have been signed along with the expiration dates.

❑ Obtain Lab Notebooks for everyone and begin following Lab Notebook procedures.

❑ Develop legal budget.

II. COMPANY FORMED BUT UNFUNDED

❑ If not already done, file patent applications.

❑ Ensure all patent applications are assigned to the Company.

❑ Consider performing a preliminary patent landscape search using a professional searcher or foreign patent office examiners.

❑ Ensure that all employees sign employment agreements which require assignment of IPR to the company; review any IP that the employee carves out as previously invented to ensure that the IP is not a part of their job function.

❑ File trademark applications domestically and internationally for key trademarks.

❑ If not already done, develop a realistic IP budget.

❑ Determine which countries outside your home country you intend to file patent applications in.

III. COMPANY FUNDED

❑ Review patent portfolio and file additional design and utility applications that may have been considered but not filed due to funding constraints.

❑ Establish ongoing competitive landscape review.

71

❑   If not already done, file trademark applications domestically and internationally.

❑   File offensive patent applications.

IV.   PRODUCT DEVELOPMENT

❑   Perform patent landscape review for product as contemplated in conjunction with product development.

❑   Perform ongoing patent landscape review to identify publishing IP that might be problematic.

V.   PRE-PRODUCT LAUNCH

❑   Perform updated patent landscape review to ensure that product is free from other IPR..

APPENDIX B

LAB NOTEBOOK PROCEDURES

- Maintain an official bound lab notebook with consecutively numbered pages.

- Enter information in permanent, water-resistant blue or black ink. [*THINK* – clearly reproducible by copier]

- Do NOT obliterate, erase or white out entries – mistakes can be lined-out but should still be readable.

- Affix print-outs (with writing on one side) in a secure manner to the lab pages – transparent
tape, permanent glue or staples – consider signing across the border of the affixed page.

- Any printout that is not permanent (e.g., thermal paper) should be photocopied *before* placing in the notebook.

- ADD a line across any portion of the page that does not have data (e.g. prior to obtaining counter-signature).

- Do NOT remove pages.

- For the US, the Lab Notebook should be kept in English.

- The person who suggested and/or carried out the work should sign and date the pages:
    - *Work of a technician performed at the direction of another should be signed by the person overseeing the work*

- A witness who is a technical person not directly involved with the work performed should review the lab notebook ("read and understand") before signing and dating.

- Consider *dual* witnesses to avoid the problem of later losing a witness' status as a result of co-inventorship.

  o *NO FURTHER ENTRIES, EXCEPT CROSS-REFERENCES TO OTHER PAGES, SHOULD BE MADE ONCE A PAGE HAS BEEN WITNESSED!*

SIGN AND DATE CONTEMPORANEOUSLY
WITNESS REGULARLY

- Memorialize:
  o *Ideas, concepts, and project goals*
  o *Further plans*
  o *Experimental procedures and details; technical paths to achieve goals*
  o *Data and technical results – contemporaneous in time and in sufficient detail to enable the work to be reproduced*
  o *Failure data; side-by-side experiments*
  o *Bases for delays on project*

- Use consistent procedures to record data.

- Avoid: editorial comments and legal conclusions.

- Key supporting documents should be signed, dated and witnessed.

APPENDIX C

SAMPLE IP STRATEGY WORKSHEET

STEP 1: Identify Market Need(s) - *what is driving product development and <u>why</u> will a customer buy the product?*

_____

STEP 2 A: **Identify Current Competitor(s) and/or Potential Acquirer(s)**

Company 1: % Market Share

Company 2: % Market Share

STEP 2B: **Outline Current Competitor(s) and/or Potential Acquirer(s)' IP Strategy**

Patents (number, type, coverage)?
Types of Patents:
❑ Utility Patent (#____)
❑ Utility Model Patent (#____)
❑ Design Patent (#____)
❑ Plant Patent (#____)
Coverage: Types of Claims
For example   ❑ Device/Apparatus
❑ Method of Operation/Use
❑ Procedure
❑ Assembly
❑ System
❑ Kits
❑ Method of Manufacture
❑ Composition
❑ Products
❑ Method of Treatment
❑ Indications of Use
Other: _____

Trademarks/ Trade Dress?

_____(number of marks, class of coverage)

75

Copyrights?

_____(registered, unregistered)

Likely Trade Secrets

_____

Sui Generis Rights[33]

_____

Countries where Registered IP (typically
patent/trademark) is often Protected:
 Usual Suspects:
  ❑ United States
  ❑ Europe
  ❑ Canada
  ❑ Australia
  ❑ Japan
  ❑ Korea
 Emerging:
  ❑ Israel
  ❑ Brazil
  ❑ Russia
  ❑ India
  ❑ China
 Others:
 _____

STEP 3A: **Identify Product/Service Market Features in
Company Products: Rate each feature from low (1) to
high (5) based on contribution to Competitive
Advantage in the Marketplace, then identify potential
IP coverage for that feature - for patents and trade
secret consider the technical improvements that
enable that feature**

POTENTIAL IP COVERAGE

_____

[33] Sui Generis Rights include: Database (Europe) / Mask Works (semi-conductor) / Plant
Variety / Supplementary Protection (pharmaceutical) / Traditional Knowledge

Market Feature(s)	Importance (1-5)	Patent Utility / Design / Plant	Trademark Trade Dress	Copyright	Trade Secret	Sui Generis

STEP 3B: Identify Primary Countries for Marketing (ranked by market size) and Manufacture - these countries should receive primary consideration for foreign filing of IP rights along with those identified in Step 2a.

Country	@ LAUNCH				Projected @ 5 Years			
	Market (Y/N)	Mfg. (Y/N)	Market Size	% Market Penetration	Market (Y/N)	Mfg. (Y/N)	Market Size	% Market Penetration
US								
Europe								
Japan								
Australia								
Canada								
Korea								
Brazil								
Russia								
India								
China								
Others?								

STEP 4: Consider Barriers to Market Entry (e.g., Regulatory, Customer Perception, etc.):

APPENDIX D

WEBSITES OF INTEREST

COPYRIGHT

American Society of Composers, Authors and Publishers: www.ascap.com
Copyright Clearance Center (rights licensing service): www.copyright.com
Copyright Office (US): www.copyright.gov
EDiMA (Europe): www.europeandigitalmedia.org
U.S. Customs IPR (copyright and trademark) recordation -
  https://www.cbp.gov/trade/priority-issues/ipr

LICENSING

Association of University Technology Managers (AUTM): www.autm.net
Licensing Executives Society (LES): www.les.org
License Stream (digital content licensing): www.licensestream.com

IP BLOGS (SELECT)

Afro IP Blog (developments in Africa): http://afro-ip.blogspot.com/
IP Kat (UK/EU): http://ipkitten.blogspot.com/
IP Tango (Latin America): http://iptango.blogspot.com/
IP Watch: http://www.ip-watch.org/
Patently-O (U.S.): http://www.patentlyo.com/
PatentlyBIOTech (US): http://patentlybiotech.wordpress.com/
Spicy IP (India): http://spicyipindia.blogspot.com/
Techno Llama: http://www.technollama.co.uk/
Tech Transfer Blog: http://techtransfercentral.com/category/tech-
transfer-enews/

PATENT

Assignment records for U.S. Patents and Pubs:
  http://assignments.uspto.gov/assignments/q?db=pat
Directory for Foreign Patent Offices:
  http://www.wipo.int/directory/en/urls.jsp
European Patent Office Online: http://www.epoline.org/

File History for U.S. Patents and Pubs on PAIR:
http://portal.uspto.gov/external/portal/pair

Free Patent Copies: http://www.freepatentsonline.com/search.html

OR   http://www.pat2pdf.org/

Google Patent Search: http://www.google.com/patents?hl=en

International (PCT Patent Search: http://www.wipo.int/pctdb/en/search-simp.jsp

IP Information for Entrepreneurs and Small Businesses (training and guidance): http://www.wipo.int/sme/en/

Patent Lens (patent searching and landscape tools): http://www.patentlens.net/daisy/patentlens/patentlens.html

Patent Search Strategies (how to): https://www.uspto.gov/learning-and-resources/support-centers/patent-and-trademark-resource-centers-ptrc/ptrc-basic

Patent Valuation Tool (IPScore) downloadable from EPO http://www.epo.org/service-support/faq/searching-patents/valuation.html#faq-148

U.S. Patent Office Overview: http://www.uspto.gov/main/patents.htm

U.S. Patent Office Searching: http://www.uspto.gov/patft/index.html

UK Patent Office: http://www.ipo.gov.uk/

WIPO IP Overview http://www.wipo.int/wipogold/en/

PATENT AUCTION SITES

Free Patent Auction: http://www.freepatentauction.com/

Ocean Tomo: http://www.oceantomo.com/

Patent Profit International http://www.patprofit.com/

Shop 4 Patents: http://www.shop4patents.com/postpat.html

PRODUCT SOLICITATION / OPEN INNOVATION WEBSITES

Clorox Company http://cloroxconnects.com/pages/0835748c9f

Glaxo Smith Kline https://innovation.gsk.com

Proctor & Gamble www.pgconnectdevelop.com

TRADEMARK

U.S. Trademark Office Overview:
http://www.uspto.gov/main/trademarks.htm

79

U.S. Customs IPR (copyright and trademark) recordation - https://www.cbp.gov/trade/priority-issues/ipr

UNIVERSITY/GOVERNMENT LICENSING SITES (SELECT)

Harvard University http://otd.harvard.edu/

Lawrence Berkeley Labs http://ipo.lbl.gov/

Stanford OTL TechFinder: http://techfinder.stanford.edu/techfinder.php

University of California http://ucop.edu/innovation-alliances-services/innovation/technology-transfer-offices/index.html

OTHER WEBSITES/ORGANIZATIONS OF INTEREST

Angel Investor Groups in Silicon Valley:

Angels Forum: www.angelsforum.com

Band of Angels: www.bandangels.com

Keiretsu Forum: (with chapters around the world) www.keiretsuforum.com

Life Science: Angels www.lifescienceangels.com

North Bay (SF) Angels: www.northbayangels.com

Sand Hill Angels: www.sandhillangels.com

Crowd Funding

Kickstarter: www.kickstarter.com

IndieGoGo: www.indiegogo.com

Peerbackers: www.peerbackers.com

GoGetFunding: www.gogetfunding.com

Financial Information:

CNBC: www.cnbc.com

Hoovers: www.hoovers.com

Yahoo Finance: www.finance.yahoo.com

Incubator Space and Prototyping Bench Facilities in Silicon Valley

Plug and Play Tech Center: www.plugandplaytechcenter.com

The Tech Shop: http://www.techshop.ws (workshop that provides members with access to tools and equipment, instruction, and a creative community) - good for prototyping.

International Government/Industry Presence in Silicon Valley

Enterprise Ireland: www.enterprise-ireland.com

Innovation Denmark: http://icdk.um.dk/

Start-up and New Business Information:

All Business: www.allbusiness.com

Entrepreneur.com: www.entrepreneur.com

Fast Company: www.fastcompany.com
Forbes: www.forbes.com
Fortune: www.fortune.com
Idea Café: www.ideacafe.com

Infoworld: www.infoworld.com

Intellectual Property Owners Org: www.ipo.org
Kauffman Foundation (Foundation of Entrepreneurship):
www.kauffman.org
Small Business Administration (SBA): www.sba.gov

Technology News and Information:
CNET: www.cnet.com
Red Herring: www.redherring.com

Silicon Valley Watcher: www.siliconvalleywatcher.com
Silicon Valley: www.siliconvalley.com

Venture Beat: www.venturebeat.com

Venture Capital Information:
Live from Silicon Valley:
www.livefromsiliconvalley.com/venture/venture.html
National Venture Capital Association: www.nvca.org

APPENDIX E

SUMMARY OF IP

IP Type	Coverage Includes	Length*	Is Registration Required?	Comments and Variations of Note
Copyright	Literary, musical, dramatic, choreographic, pictorial, graphic, sculptural, audiovisual, smell, and sound records	Minimum term of 50 years from publication or life of author plus 50 years[34] The actual term can be longer in a jurisdiction.	None for rights to attach; may be required to enforce	Some countries recognize a moral right of authors that is separate from the economic right of the current owner. Marking is advisable. Marking includes, at a minimum, © [Year(s)] [Owner Name - individual or company], e.g. © 2010 John Smith.

---

[34] Berne Convention, Article 7

IP Type	Coverage Includes	Length*	Is Registration Required?	Comments and Variations of Note
Patent Types				
Utility	New, useful, and non-obvious improvements in an article of manufacture	20 years from earliest effective filing date[35]	Yes	Countries can exclude coverage for some categories of invention based on public policy, such as surgical treatments. Marking impacts notice to potential infringers and may be advisable.
Design	New and original ornamental (as opposed to useful) features that make an article attractive and appealing to a potential purchaser	Up to 15 years	Yes	Design patents are a useful complement to utility protection particularly for medical device inventions. Marking impacts notice to potential infringers and may be advisable.

---

[35] TRIPs Agreement, Article 33.

IP Type	Coverage Includes	Length*	Is Registration Required?	Comments and Variations of Note
Utility Model†‡	Similar to a utility patent but usually less stringent patentability requirements and a shorter term	7-10 years	Yes	Also referred to as "petty patent" or "short term patent." Can be a good strategic complement in countries where there is significant R&D or sales, or in countries with emerging economies. Marking impacts notice to potential infringers and may be advisable.
Plant	Asexually reproduced plant varieties	20 years from earliest effective filing date for plant patents	Yes	

IP Type	Coverage Includes	Length*	Is Registration Required?	Comments and Variations of Note
Sui Generis	Legal classification of rights that exists independent of other categorizations mentioned above.			
Databases†‡	Protects from copying and dissemination of information in a database	15 years		Limited availability: first introduced in Europe In Europe, the term is re-calculated upon substantial new investment in verification or editing.
Mask Works†	Protects two or three-dimensional layout or topography of an integrated circuit	10 years in the US	Yes (in the US)	General Agreement on Trade and Tariffs (GATT), Trade-Related Aspects of Intellectual Property Rights (TRIPs) requires that substantial parts of the IPIC Treaty be followed by member countries.

IP Type	Coverage Includes	Length*	Is Registration Required?	Comments and Variations of Note
Plant Variety Protection/ Plant Breeder's Rights	Rights granted to breeders of new plant varieties that give them control over the propagating material; new sexually reproduced and tuber-propagated varieties	minimum of 15 years under UPOV[36]	Yes	May be excluded from coverage in some jurisdictions.
Supplementary Protection Certificates/ Patent Term Extension†	Extends the patent term for patents covering human medicinal product for which data from clinical trials was required or plant protection products (pesticides)	Varies depending upon, for example, delay in time for obtaining permission to sell the product	Yes	Note that in the U.S. additional patent term may be provided for regulatory delay.

---

[36] UPOV, Portugal Decree, Law 213/90, Article 4.

IP Type	Coverage Includes	Length*	Is Registration Required?	Comments and Variations of Note
Traditional/ Indigenous Knowledge and Medicine†‡	A term used to identify indigenous peoples' special rights to claim their indigenous know-how	None yet		There has been an increased call for an IPR mechanism to protect traditional knowledge. This is one of the sui generis areas that should be monitored for increased activity. For example, on the national stage some countries have instituted a requirement that the source of materials be identified in utility patent applications relying on source materials (e.g., for biotech inventions).

IP Type	Coverage Includes	Length*	Is Registration Required?	Comments and Variations of Note
Trade Dress	Protects the distinctive non-functional features of packaging/presentation of a product or service that identifies the products or services in commerce	10 years	Yes	In the U.S. trade dress is covered by trademark law. In foreign countries it may be protected under unfair competition law.
Trademark / Service Mark	Words, slogan, design, picture, symbols, smells, and the like that are used to identify and distinguish goods and services in commerce	10 years	Not strictly required in common law countries, but recommended	Rights in common law countries can arise initially from usage; in countries that follow code law, rights arise with government registration but in some jurisdictions a trademark owner may be able to argue rights arising through distinctiveness and use. Marking with TM (prior to registration) and ® (after registration) advisable.

IP Type	Coverage Includes	Length*	Is Registration Required?	Comments and Variations of Note
Trade Secret	Business information that has economic value which is subjected to reasonable efforts to preserve its confidentiality	Indefinite	No	Does not protect against independent discovery or reverse engineering.

*Term can vary by jurisdiction
†Not available in all jurisdictions
‡Not available in the United States

APPENDIX F

SAMPLE INNOVATION DISCLOSURE FORM

INNOVATION DISCLOSURE

Instructions: The information contained in this document is **CONFIDENTIAL** and should not be disclosed to others without prior authorization or without a Confidentiality Agreement (or Non Disclosure Agreement) in place. Submit this disclosure to your **Innovation Disclosure Coordinator or Patent Attorney/Agent** as soon as possible.

No patent protection is possible until a patent application is authorized, prepared, and submitted to the Patent Office.

EFFECTIVE MARCH 16, 2013,
THE UNITED STATES OPERATES ON A FIRST-TO-FILE BASIS.

Descriptive Title of Innovation:
Name of Project (if applicable):
Product Name (if known):
Was a description or image of the innovation published (*e.g.,* in a journal, in a society abstract, on the Internet, or elsewhere), or are you planning to publish a description of the innovation? ☐ YES // ☐ NO If YES, the date(s), publication (s), and available citation information: _____ *Please also provide a copy of the publication (or draft publication), if available.* Was a product that includes the innovation announced (*e.g.* in a Press Release or Tweet), offered for sale, or sold? ☐ YES // ☐ NO Or is such activity proposed? If YES, the date(s) and location(s): _____ Was the innovation disclosed, demonstrated or shown to anyone not subject to a Confidentiality Agreement (*e.g.,* outside of the company), or will such disclosure occur? ☐ YES // ☐ NO If YES, the date(s) and name(s):

If any of the above situations will occur contact your Innovation Coordinator or Patent Attorney ASAP!

Was the innovation described in a lab notebook or other written record?
　　☐ YES // ☐ NO
　　If YES, please identify (lab book #, location of documents, etc.) and attach copies of those pages.

　　What was the date the invention was first conceived (if not the date of the earliest written record)? _____

Was the innovation built or tested? ☐ YES // ☐ NO

　　If YES, the date on which the device was built and/or tested

_____

Has the innovation been used for any purpose other than testing? ☐ YES // ☐ NO

　　If YES, describe the purpose:

　　_____

Was this innovation made under a government grant, contract or proposal?

　　☐ YES // ☐ NO

　　If YES, the agency and contract number: _____

　　Was/Is the grant or proposal a public submission? ☐ YES // ☐ NO

[Date on which it became/becomes public _____]

Was this innovation made under a joint research agreement, development agreement, consulting agreement or in cooperation or collaboration with another person or company?
　　☐ YES // ☐ NO
　　If YES, the name of the person or company :

Do any of the inventors live outside the United States? OR, was any part of the invention developed outside the United States (*e.g.* in collaboration by fax and/or email)? ☐ YES // ☐ NO If YES, which countries? _____
Are there any aspects of this invention that *cannot* be reverse engineered? ☐ YES // ☐ NO If YES, which aspects? _____ Additional information on **Appendix A**: ☐ Yes// ☐ No

Has a regulatory filing (*e.g.*, US FDA 510k, IDE, PMA) been made which relies on or references predicate device(s) or products?   ☐ Yes// ☐ No// ☐ N/A
    If YES, please provide a list of all predicate devices or products along with information in your possession regarding the device(s) or products.
 	
    Please also provide the name of the person most knowledgeable about the regulatory filings: _____

Can all or part of this innovation be incorporated into another device or apparatus?   ☐ Yes// ☐ No
If the innovation involves **SOFTWARE**, does it produce a technical effect (e.g. changes the workings of an apparatus, changes a product or process)?   ☐ Yes// ☐ No *If YES, please describe:* Additional information on **Appendix A**: ☐ Yes// ☐ No
Can all or part of this innovation be configured to be part of a **communication network** (*e.g.*, diagnostic information or measurement that is communicated to a central location)?   ☐ Yes// ☐ No Additional information attached: ☐ Yes// ☐ No

*For **SOFTWARE** patents, if the invention is directed to an "abstract idea" it is not eligible for utility patent coverage. Abstract ideas include:*
    • *Fundamental economic practices (such as how to hedge risk)*
    • *Certain methods of organizing human activities*
    • *An idea itself*
    • *Mathematical relationships / formulas (such as a formula for converting*

binary coded numerals into pure binary form)
- *Collecting and analyzing data - without more*

The subject matter may be patent eligible if we can establish:
- *The invention improves another technology or technical field*
- *The invention improves the functioning of the computer itself*
- *Detail on how information is transformed (e.g., algorithm that is applied)*

Can all or part of this innovation be configured to be part of a **communication network** (*e.g.*, diagnostic information or measurement that is communicated to a central location)?

❑ Yes// ❑ No

Additional information attached: ❑ Yes// ❑ No

Is there any secondary application that would be useful to, for example, NASA, Department of Energy, CIA or any other governmental agency having investment funds?

❑ Yes// ❑ No

OPTIONAL: Which markets do you think will be the target key markets for the product?

OPTIONAL: Which countries would a likely competitor make and/or sell a competing product?

OPTIONAL: Who are the competitors or potential acquirers?

Please describe any human factors (or usability) details that went into the design of the product:

Does this disclosure include a **DESIGN** contemplated for the commercial embodiment of the product (note that design applications can be filed for GUIs)?
❑ Yes// ❑ No

If YES, should a design patent application also be filed ? ❑ Yes// ❑ No

If YES, please identify figures corresponding to one or more commercial devices:

Description of Innovation: *Please preserve all records of the innovation and attach additional pages for the following. Each additional page should be signed and dated by the innovator(s) and witness(es). Witnesses should be persons who understand the innovation but are not innovators.*

A.   Prior solutions and their disadvantages (if available, attach copies of product literature, technical articles, patents, etc.).

B.   Problems solved by the innovation.

C.   Advantages of the innovation over what has been done before.

D.   Description of the construction and operation of the innovation (include appropriate schematic, block, & timing diagrams; drawings; samples; graphs; flowcharts; computer listings; test results; etc.) For the description, consider the following categories:

    I.   Device(s) – the actual device itself, if applicable

    II.   Method of Operation – the way the device or software is used, if applicable

    III.   Method of Treatment – how a person is treated – *not available in all countries*

    IV.   Kits – if the device or components can be part of a kit (think razor blades)

    V.   Method of Manufacture – how is the device manufactured

    VI.   Composition, Products, Second Medical Use, etc.

    VII.   Assay/Tool claims

E.   Features that are likely to influence a potential customer to purchase a product manufactured under a patent filed from this disclosure.

F.   Consider how a competitor might attempt to incorporate this innovation into their own product and/or design around this innovation

Signature of Innovators(s): I (we) hereby submit this disclosure on this date: [_____].

Innovator-1			
	Full Legal Name	Signature	Date
Innovator-2			
	Full Legal Name	Signature	Date
Innovator-3			
	Full Legal Name	Signature	Date
Innovator-4			
	Full Legal Name	Signature	Date

❏ *There are more than* FOUR *innovators, detailed information about additional innovator(s) is listed in* **Appendix A.**

Signature of Witness(es): *(Try to obtain the signature of the person(s) to whom innovation was first disclosed.)*
The innovation was first explained to, and understood by, me (us) on this date:
[_____]

Witness-1			
	Full Legal Name	Signature	Date
Witness-2			
	Full Legal Name	Signature	Date

Innovator & Home Address Information: *(If more than four innovators, include addl. information on a copy of this form & attach to this document)*

For Each Innovator Provide		
	Innovator's Full Legal Name (As It Should Appear on the Patent)	
	Innovator's Home Address: Street Address	
	City	
	State	
	Zip	
	Citizenship	
	Work Phone	
	Mobile Phone	
	Email address	
	Residential P.O. Address (if applicable)? P.O. Box	
	City	
	State	
	Zip	

APPENDIX G

SAMPLE INNOVATION DISCLOSURE FORM

INNOVATION DISCLOSURE

DESIGN
NONFUNCTIONAL ASPECTS OF AN ORNAMENTAL DESIGN

Instructions: The information contained in this document is **CONFIDENTIAL** and should not be disclosed to others without prior authorization or without a Confidentiality Agreement (or Non Disclosure Agreement) in place. Submit this disclosure to your **Innovation Disclosure Coordinator or Patent Attorney/Agent** as soon as possible.

No patent protection is possible until a patent application is authorized, prepared, and submitted to the Patent Office.
EFFECTIVE MARCH 16, 2013,
THE UNITED STATES OPERATES ON A FIRST-TO-FILE BASIS.

Descriptive Title of Design:
Name of Project (if applicable):
Product Name (if known):
Was a description or image of the design published (*e.g.,* in a journal, in a society abstract, on the Internet, or elsewhere), or are you planning to publish a description of the design? ☐ YES // ☐ NO If YES, the date(s), publication (s), and available citation information: _____ *Please also provide a copy of the publication (or draft publication), if available.*
Was a product that includes the design announced (*e.g.* in a Press Release or Tweet), offered for sale, or sold? ☐ YES // ☐ NO Or is such activity proposed? If YES, the date(s) and location(s): _____
Was the design disclosed, demonstrated or shown to anyone who WAS NOT subject to a Confidentiality Agreement (*e.g.*, outside of the company), or will such disclosure occur? ☐ YES // ☐ NO

If YES, the date(s) and name(s):
_____
Was the design disclosed, demonstrated or shown to anyone who WAS subject to a Confidentiality Agreement (*e.g.*, outside of the company or with a vertical integration partner), or will such disclosure occur? ☐ YES // ☐ NO
If YES, the date(s) and name(s):
_____
If any of the above situations will occur contact your Innovation Coordinator or Patent Attorney ASAP!
Was the design described in a lab notebook or other written record? ☐ YES // ☐ NO
If YES, please identify (lab book #, location of documents, etc.) and attach copies of those pages.
What was the date the design was first conceived (if not the date of the earliest written record)? _____
Was a product of the design built or tested? ☐ YES // ☐ NO
If YES, the date on which the device was built _____ and/or tested _____
Is the design primarily ornamental (as opposed to functional)? ☐ YES // ☐ NO
Note: the design must be ornamental in order to satisfy the subject matter requirement. If the design is primarily functional, then the requirement will not be met.
Was this design made under a government grant, contract or proposal? ☐ YES // ☐ NO
If YES, the agency and contract number: _____
Was/Is the grant or proposal a public submission? ☐ YES // ☐ NO
[Date on which it became/becomes public _____]

Was this design made under a joint research agreement, development agreement, consulting agreement or in cooperation or collaboration with another person or company?

☐ YES // ☐ NO

If YES, the name of the person or company :

Do any of the inventors live outside the United States? OR, was any part of the invention developed outside the United States (*e.g.* in collaboration by fax and/or email)?

☐ YES // ☐ NO

If YES, which countries?

_____

OPTIONAL: Which markets do you think will be the target key markets for the product?

OPTIONAL: Which countries would a likely competitor make and/or sell a competing product using this design?

OPTIONAL: Who are the competitors or potential acquirers?

Please provide one or more images of the design. For example, a device design should include a perspective view, a front view, a back view, left and right side views and top and bottom views. Software interfaces should include one or more screen shots of the interface or icon to be protected.

Description of the Design: *Please describe the various images illustrating the design which are provided. Please mark any features which are not intended to be claimed in the design.*

Signature of Innovators(s): I (we) hereby submit this disclosure on this date: [_____].

| **Innovator-1** | _____ |
| | Full Legal Name Signature   Date |

| **Innovator-2** | _____ |
| | Full Legal Name Signature   Date |

❑ *There are more than TWO innovators.*	

Signature of Witness(es): *(Try to obtain the signature of the person(s) to whom the innovation was first disclosed and who are not inventors.)*
The innovation was first explained to, and understood by, me (us) on this date:
[_____]

Witness-1	Full Legal Name Signature	Date
Witness-2	Full Legal Name Signature	Date

Innovator & Home Address Information: *(If more than four innovators, include addl. information on a copy of this form & attach to this document)*

For Each Innovator Provide	Innovator's Full Legal Name (As It Should Appear on the Patent)	
	Innovator's Home Address: Street Address	
	City	
	State	
	Zip	
	Citizenship	
	Work Phone	
	Mobile Phone	
	Email address	
	Residential P.O. Address (if applicable)? P.O. Box	
	City	
	State	
	Zip	

APPENDIX H

SAMPLE TIME LINES FOR PATENT FILINGS

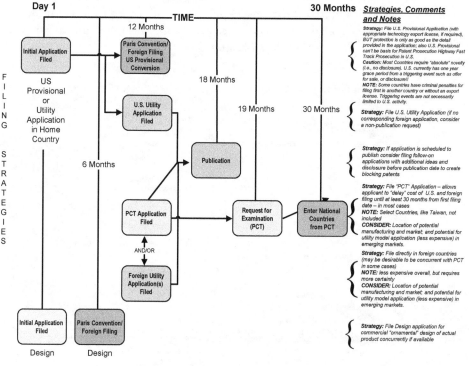

APPENDIX I

ANATOMY OF A PATENT REFERENCE

The face of a patent reference can often provide valuable information. Currently, patent applications and issued patents are published with codes for each of the fields. Note that the coded fields do not necessarily appear in the same location and that not all fields will appear in all publications.

(12) **United States Patent**
Breen

(10) Patent No.: **US 7,502,641 B2**
(45) **Date of Patent:** **Mar. 10, 2009**

(54) **METHOD FOR IMAGING THE RELATIVE MOTION OF SKELETAL SEGMENTS**

(75) Inventor: **Alan Breen**, Christchurch (GB)

(73) Assignee: **AECC Enterprises Limited**, Bournemouth (GB)

(*) Notice: Subject to any disclaimer, the term of this patent is extended or adjusted under 35 U.S.C. 154(b) by 168 days.

(21) Appl. No.: **10/520,489**

(22) PCT Filed: **Jul. 8, 2003**

(86) PCT No.: **PCT/GB03/02934**
§ 371 (c)(1),
(2), (4) Date: **Jan. 7, 2005**

(87) PCT Pub. No.: **WO2004/004570**
PCT Pub. Date: **Jan. 15, 2004**

(65) **Prior Publication Data**
US 2005/0259794 A1   Nov. 24, 2005

(30) **Foreign Application Priority Data**
Jul. 9, 2002   (GB) 0215848.3
Nov. 11, 2002   (GB) 0226264.0

(51) **Int. Cl.**
A61B 5/05 (2006.01)
A47B 13/08 (2006.01)

(52) **U.S. Cl.** 600/415; 5/601; 600/410; 600/436

(58) **Field of Classification Search** 600/410, 600/415, 422; 5/601
See application file for complete search history.

(56) **References Cited**

U.S. PATENT DOCUMENTS

5,090,042 A	2/1992	Bejjani et al.
5,099,859 A	3/1992	Bell
5,320,640 A	6/1994	Riddle et al.
5,445,152 A	8/1995	Bell et al.

(Continued)

FOREIGN PATENT DOCUMENTS

EP   0 804 032 A2   10/1997

(Continued)

OTHER PUBLICATIONS

Breen et al., "Quantitative Analysis Of Lumbar Spine Intersegmental Motion," *European Journal Of Physical Medicine And Rehabilitation*, 1993, vol. 3, No. 5, pp. 182-190.

(Continued)

Primary Examiner—Eric F Winakur
Assistant Examiner—Helene Bor
(74) *Attorney, Agent, or Firm*—Cecily Ann O'Regan; Wilson Sonsini Goodrich & Rosati

(57) **ABSTRACT**

Methods and apparatus for measuring the movement of bones during joint motion in a subject using a motion table, an imaging device, and software program for tracking, calculating and graphing the results of the motion study. The apparatus is a motion table used to control the movement of the subject while an imaging device captures images during that movement. The images are analyzed using a computer software program that tracks the individual bones that make up the joint, calculates their relative movements, and graphically displays the results as a function of time.

24 Claims, 8 Drawing Sheets

Passive Motion Platform - Side Elevation

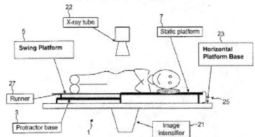

101

An explanation of select codes appearing on US publications and PCT Publications are as follows:

(*)   Notice regarding terminal disclaimer or patent term extension in the US

(10)   Reference number (e.g., patent number, publication number), currently starts with the two digit country code and ends with a refence code ("kind code") which the country publishing has identified as having a particular meaning

The PCT Publishes the two digit country codes at:
http://www.wipo.int/pct/guide/en/gdvol1/annexes/annexk/ax_k.pdf

In the US, for example, kind code A1 is a published application, B1 is an issued patent which does not have a prior publication, and B2 is an issued patent which does have a prior publication.

(12)   Country publishing the application or patent

(21)   Application number. In the US the application number is a combination of a series number and a serial number. The series number (e.g., "10/" is another way to identify the type of application filed)

(22)   PCT Filing date – where the application is a national stage of a PCT application

(25)   Filing language

(26)   Published language

(30)   Priority data – the earlier filed applications that are the basis of the filed application. In the US, for example, these earlier filed applications are foreign priority applications under the Paris Convention but are not used for purposes of calculating the patent term

(45)   The date of publication

(51)   International Classification – the classification that the Examiner used for purposes of examining the application. For a particular relevant reference, the classification can be used as part of the searching strategy. Note that

where more than one classification is provided, any bolded classifications are considered the most relevant.

(52) US Classification – the classification that the Examiner used for purposes of examining the application. Note that where more than one classification is provided, any bolded classifications are considered the most relevant.

(54) The title of the application or patent

(56) References cited. For an issued US patent, the references cited and considered by the Examiner are listed organized by type of reference: US Patent Documents, Foreign Patent Documents and Other Publications (also referred to as "O-Refs" or NPL (Non-patent Literature). Any reference that includes an "*" is a reference that was cited by the Examiner and therefore likely considered more relevant.

(57) The Abstract is a short summary of what is disclosed.

(58) Field of Classification Search

(60) Provisional patent application(s). In the US, this application is often used for internal priority of a filing. The date of any patent term is NOT calculated from the provisional filing date.

(65) Prior publication data, e.g., earlier US publication date for an issued US patent

(71) The applicant
Until recently the applicant in the US was the inventors. The US now allows for the international practice of listing the owner as the applicant, which means the assignee can be listed as applicant

(72) The inventor(s)

(73) The assignee (or owner)

(74) Legal representative and contact information

(75) The inventors and applicants

(81)   Designated States for national protection available from the PCT

(84)   Designated States for regional protection available from the PCT (e.g. European Patent Office, etc.)

(86)   PCT Application Number – in the US this information includes the 371(c)(1) date that the application entered the national stage into the US

(87)   PCT Publication Number and Publication Date

(88)   Date of publication of the search report – the search report can be useful in understanding which references were considered relevant by the examiner for a particular published patent document.

INDEX